9/12

D0638324

BOOMERANGNATION

How to Survive Living with Your Parents...
The Second Time Around

ELINAFURMAN

A Fireside Book
Published by Simon & Schuster

New York   London   Toronto   Sydney

FIRESIDE
Rockefeller Center
1230 Avenue of the Americas
New York, NY 10020

FIRESIDE and colophon are registered trademarks
of Simon & Schuster, Inc.

For information regarding special discounts for bulk purchases,
please contact Simon & Schuster Special Sales at 1-800-456-6798
or business@simonandschuster.com

Designed by Ruth Lee-Mui

Manufactured in the United States of America

1   3   5   7   9   10   8   6   4   2

Library of Congress Cataloging-in-Publication Data

Furman, Elina.
Boomerang nation : how to survive living with your parents
. . . the second time around / Elina Furman.
p.   cm.
1. Adult children living with parents—United States.
2. Parent and adult child—United States.   3. Adult children—
United States—Psychology.   I. Title.

HQ799.97.U5F87   2005
646.7'8'0842—dc22   2005040613

ISBN 0-7432-6991-8

ISBN 978-0-7432-6991-9

For Mom

If it hadn't been for all your
love and dedication,
I might have left home a lot sooner.

CONTENTS

BOOMERANGNATION

THE BOOMERANGER
IN THE BASEMENT

Shhh!

It's happening all over the country. A quiet revolution has been brewing. Look around and you'll see signs everywhere. It's not just your imagination. Others are beginning to notice, too. Something is happening, something is coming in greater numbers than you could possibly imagine. Millions, maybe even tens of millions, are coming out in droves.

No, it's not the every-seventeen-year emergence of the cicada population. These are people we're talking about, ordinary citizens like you and me. "Who are these strange, fascinating creatures?" you may be asking. They go by many different names: "boomerangers," "nesters," "homebounders," "twixters"—you name it. And according to the U.S. Census Bureau, their numbers are 18 million strong and growing.

Until recently, most boomerangers had to suffer in silence. Cut off from the world with no access to communication channels or social networks, they were forced to subsist on bad daytime television, leftovers, and their parents' pestering. Living in virtual bubbles of isolation, many boomerangers had no idea that there were others like them out there.

It didn't help that no one wanted to talk about it, either. When asked how their grown kids were doing, parents of boomerangers would mumble and look the other way. Refusing to break their code of silence, they lived in perpetual fear that one day their nosy next-door neighbor would uncover their dirty little secret: that they, indeed, had a boomeranger in the basement. Treated as second-class citizens, boomerangers felt shackled and misunderstood as they struggled to combat an overwhelming sense of alienation, loneliness, and anxiety.

Until one day, the silence was shattered.

Reports began to surface with increasing frequency. Scientists and sociologists got into the game as well, launching full-scale studies and reports about the boomeranger population. Pretty soon, the word had spread. Millions of young adults were living at home. Tired of hiding out in the family's closets, basements, and attics, boomerangers sprang out of their self-imposed traps with a resounding battle cry. Suddenly, they were everywhere—daytime talk shows, reality TV, national newspapers, and on the big screen. Boomerangers had finally come out of the basement. No longer would they be intimidated or belittled.

With all this talk about moving back home, there's an even more important question at hand: What if you never left? Think about it. All of us leave the nest at some time, but what if there's no clear, definitive break from family life to independence? There are the weekend trips to your family's house, nightly dinners there, and days spent just hanging out in the backyard. Even if we did move into our own apartments, some of us never left emotionally. In my case, I never left—period.

It all started when I graduated from college. With no job and no desire to learn the art of making mocha lattes at the local Starbucks, I moved back to my family home in Highland Park, Illinois. And before you start picturing my parents as this happy wonderful couple, let me interject by telling you that *no*, we weren't the picture of domestic bliss. My parents were in the middle of a difficult divorce. So there we all were—me, my soon-to-be-divorced parents, and my older sister. Talk about dysfunction!

As soon as the house was sold, my mom, sister, and I packed up; we were off to move into a new condo in Chicago. You might ask why I would be so quick to move back in with my mother and sister after being stuck for so long together. Well, my mom and I have always been close and I was very worried about her living on her own. As much as I told myself that she would be scared living by herself, I realized I was even more nervous, and the same was probably true of my sister. So all three of us set off on the new adventure, more roommates and friends by now than nagging family members.

I have to say that for a while there, living with my mom and sister was really a lot of fun. Since my mother had never lived solo, we all felt as if we were on our own for the very first time. On our own, but together. We stayed up talking until all hours of the night, took European vacations together, and ate chocolate cake for breakfast. I was able to quit my day job and work full-time as a writer.

Fast-forward to five years later, and things had gone from great to not so good. A move from Chicago to New York didn't go quite as planned. Our three-bedroom condo in Chicago turned into a small two-bedroom apartment in New York, my writing assignments started dwindling, and my seven-year relationship with my now ex-boyfriend went kaput two days before the September 11 terrorist attacks. I was agitated, depressed, and, at 29, wondering how in the world I'd ended up living with my mother and sister for so long.

All those years had passed, and I was right back where I started—or so it seemed to me at the time. All those published books, TV appearances, newspaper articles, and I had somehow become a cautionary tale; an example of what *not* do rather than the proactive and motivated person I used to be. Questions like "What's wrong with me?" "Will I always be so immature?" Why can't I just move on with my life?" plagued me on a daily basis. It's no wonder my mother, sister, and I began fighting more often. Something had to give. As much as we were scared to change the status quo, I think all of us were ready to move on. And while I still had no answers, no direction, and no idea what I was going to do with the rest of my life, one thing was certain. I would have to do it on my own.

In the end, I wrote this book as much for myself as for all of you. Believe me, I needed to hear the stories that you'll find in this book as much you do. After years of cohabitating with my mother and sister, I finally took the plunge and moved out. Let's just say Mom took it kind of hard. No matter how much I tried to motivate and encourage her, she just wasn't ready to live on her own. So to help her ease through the transition and allay her anxiety, I began doing research on empty nesters. I found hundreds of articles about parents who have a hard time letting go, and that's when it happened. I stumbled on one article about a group called "Boomerang Kids."

I stared transfixed at it. Here I was thinking I was the only person in the free world who still lived with her mom, only to find out that there were millions of people out there who were doing the same thing. You can imagine my shock, surprise, and immense relief. It was like waking up alone in a post-apocalyptic world only to find out you're not the sole survivor. I was saved. I was normal. There were others out there!

That's when I started thinking about all of those other boomerangers—all of *you!* I wondered if the news had reached you. I thought about whether you had any idea of what was going on, and worried that many of you were laboring under the same misconception that I had been. That's when I decided I *had* to write this book. Not only would I be able to impart some of the lessons I had learned, I could find out if other boomerangers had the same feelings, insecurities, and concerns that I did.

Part of the reason so many of us were struggling is that to some extent, we all felt disenfranchised, alone, and alienated from the rest of the world. After all, no one was really championing our voices or standing up for our rights. We needed to band together—and fast! I wanted this book to start a dialogue that would get us talking about the trials and tribulations of living at home as an adult, and ultimately answer some of the pressing questions that defied easy explanations. Questions like:

➐ Is anyone ever completely independent?
➐ Does moving back home mean I'm a failure?
➐ What does it mean to be a mature adult?

- Does living at home stunt my emotional and psychological growth?
- Why do I feel so much stigma and shame for needing my family's support?
- And finally, doesn't choosing my own way, my own lifestyle, make me more independent than just doing what's expected?

There simply wasn't any information to validate our feelings and answer the many burning questions we had about moving back in with our parents. So with all the myths and misconceptions floating around, I set out to write a book that would set the record straight once and for all.

Whether you're struggling to climb out from under a mountain of debt, have returned home after a relationship setback, or are recently unemployed, this book will help you find concrete, prescriptive and field-tested strategies for improving life at home and moving toward independence.

You'll find tips on things like dealing with parents, battling depression, and getting out of debt, and will read stories from boomerangers like yourself who have struggled with parental pressure, societal expectations, and their secret fears about being stuck in a precarious state somewhere between youth and adulthood. You'll also find plans to help you begin to take the necessary steps toward economic and emotional independence.

Since many of you are probably struggling to cope with parents, you'll find guidelines for dealing with different types of parents as well as how to solve the most common relating problems when you're living at home. Getting along with adult siblings will likely rank high on your list as well, so I've included strategies that will help you deal with each other as adults rather than the bickering childhood rivals you once were. You'll also learn all about how to handle the day-to-day reality of living at home, such as dividing chores, setting boundaries, and dealing with privacy issues.

Once you've worked out the kinks with your family, you'll need to take some time to work on your social, financial, and professional lives. Since many of you come home to recuperate from setbacks in these areas, rest assured you'll find plenty of valuable advice from boomerangers like yourself who've used their time at home to regroup, redirect, and recharge. Some of the topics we'll cover include: how to talk about living at home with prospective dates, how to meet new friends when you're stuck in the suburbs, how to start from scratch during a career transition, and how to afford graduate school when you can't afford toothpaste.

By eliminating the stigma of moving in with your parents and showing that you're not alone (not by a long shot), this book should provide some of the hope and assurance many of you sorely need. So whether you're still weighing your options or have already boomeranged back to the family nest, you'll find what you need to make the transition as smooth as possible.

In the end, despite all the naysayers who will tell you that living at home at your age is abnormal, regressive, or just plain weird, you'll have to be the final judge. After all, what do they know? it's not like you woke up one morning and decided to go broke, lose your job, and then move in with Mom and Dad.

So when in doubt, remember: It's your life! Once you start listening to your own voice, even if it contradicts everything your friends, parents, and boss want you to think, you'll realize that moving back home as an adult is *not* a sign of failure. It is, in fact, an indicator of sound financial planning that can help you forge a satisfying lifestyle on your own terms.

Welcome home!

1

BOOMERANGERS UNITE!

After school, my parents didn't blink an eye when I told them I'd be moving back home. They kind of just shrugged their shoulders and handed over the garage-door opener. It's funny, because I remember how different things were for my older sister eight years ago. When she wanted to move home, my parents freaked. They thought she had lost her mind, that she was having some kind of nervous breakdown. They even blamed themselves for being horrible parents. I think it helps that a lot of their friends now have their kids living at home, too. They're much cooler about it now.

—Amanda, 24, Arlington, VA

Good news! Most people moving home today will find that the stigma of living at home has all but disappeared. Having come out of the basement, boomerangers are proud, loud, and not afraid to show the world that they mean business. With so many young adults opting to return to the nest around the world, it's become clear that we boomerangers are not going away anytime soon.

While there may not have been any overnight breakthroughs, there has been a slow and gradual acceptance of boomeranging. Over the years, the nuclear American family has evolved to the point where we can barely recognize ourselves, steadily morphing into a model European family, where multiple generations live and even thrive together under one roof.

What used to be seen as a social taboo has now become a commonly accepted life passage. Attitudes have significantly changed, bringing with them an entirely new way of looking at adulthood. No longer do we set a rigid timeline for how long it takes to mature, establish a rewarding career, or start a family. And judging by this chart, it's clear that many of us aren't in any rush to get to the finish line. According to the 2000 census:

1970	12.5 million 18- to 34-year-olds live at home.
2000	17.8 million 18- to 34-year-olds live at home.

Going by the sheer size of this demographic, it's clear that boomerangers can't be pigeonholed into one neat stereotype. They come in all shapes and sizes, from a variety of socioeconomic backgrounds and cultures, and are equally diverse in their views about what brought on the sudden change in their lifestyles.

Sociologists, economists, and psychologists have been scratching their heads, analyzing various statistics to figure out what brought about this unexpected shift. And after much research and painstaking data collection, the following emerged as some of the main contributors to the explosive boomerang phenomenon.

- Financial problems, like high credit card and school loan debt
- A tight job market and lack of opportunities for recent graduates
- A reluctance to grow up and accept adult responsibilities
- A delay in the average age for marriage for both men and women
- The prohibitive cost of housing
- Illness or death of parent
- Breakup or divorce
- Close, best-friend-like relationships between parents and young adults
- Multiculturalism and its emphasis on intergenerational living

IT'S THE ECONOMY, STUPID!

The American Dream is not what it used to be. According to recent statistics fewer and fewer high-school-age children expect to have it better than their parents. And with good reason. In light of the recent recession, the high unemployment rate, and the exorbitant cost of housing, most of us consider ourselves pretty lucky just to be able to squat at our parents' place after we graduate or find a pink slip where the holiday bonus should have been.

The 1990s saw many of our hopes rise and fall in the span of five years. When the technology sector was booming, companies couldn't seem to create new positions fast enough. The rallying cry was "Hire, hire, hire!" But with the dot-com bust of 2001, the same companies changed their tune to "Fire, fire, fire!"

The Bureau of Labor Statistics reported that 10.9 percent of 20- to 24-year-olds were unemployed in September 2003, versus 6.7 percent in September 2000. The jobless rate for 25- to 34-year-olds rose as well, from 3.7 to 6.3 percent in that same period.

> One day I was living the good life, really good, and then everything crashed. I had about half a million in options and then I was down to zero—overnight! Suddenly, I couldn't afford anything. It was good-bye shopping, good-bye expense account, good-bye weekly manicures and pedicures, good-bye apartment. Months went by and I still couldn't find work. I finally broke down and took a part-time at a clothing store (something I swore I would never do). But there was no way I could afford to live in the city on what I was making. Luckily, my parents lived close by and took pity on me. I honestly don't know what I would have done if it wasn't for them.
>
> —Lesley, 27, Austin, TX

Simply put, the middle-class lifestyle of our parents that seemed so readily attainable has gradually revealed itself as a mirage in our new economy. All the fruits we expected as our birthright—cars, houses, health insurance, job stability—now seem like relics of an idealized and out-of-reach past.

CASH PAD

Anyone who's ever thumbed a nose at the younger generations for being shiftless, aimless, and incapable of supporting themselves clearly never experienced the degradation of answering an ad for a $1,000-per-month apartment only to find a hovel with no windows, heating, or fridge. While bustling cities like New York, Chicago, and San Francisco beckon to recent graduates with the promise of greater opportunities, culture, and creative fervor, these very same environs are virtually uninhabitable for anyone making under $40,000 or $50,000 a year (and let's face it, most starting salaries are far lower).

Sure, we often hear of young people living like sardines in up-and-coming neighborhoods and eating ramen noodles by candlelight. But when faced with the prospect of shelling out more than half of their monthly salary for a fraction of the amenities, many young adults are opting out of the shabby chic living phase in favor of the plush and comfy confines of their family homes.

Not only are skyrocketing rental prices squeezing us out, but the housing sales market is equally unwelcoming. Chew on this: The National Association of Realtors estimated that the cost of a home rose by 500 percent, from 1973 to 2004, to a median price of $156,200. Not only that, the typical starter household income for that same time period increased only 300 percent, to an average of $42,228. What does it all mean? It means that our salaries just can't keep pace with the rising cost of housing, and many of us feel that there's no way we'll ever be able to experience the dream of home ownership. Unless, of course, we save for a down payment by moving home with Mom and Dad.

Take Stan, for example. After graduating with an MBA from a top school, he moved to San Francisco to start his mid-six-figure-salary job. Stan could have had his pick of any number of deluxe apartments overlooking the city. Instead, he opted to move home with his parents for two years in order to pay off his $75,000 school loan and start saving to buy a place of his own.

> I figured if my parents were cool enough to give me a free ride by letting me crash at home, I could pay down my school debt in a couple of years. That's pretty good if you think about it. If I really buckled down and saved, I could even scrape a little bit toward a down payment on a condo. If I had moved straight into my own apartment, it would probably take me more like eight to ten years to get to that same point. I figure it was a compromise worth making.
>
> —Stan, 28, Santa Rosa, CA

It may feel like a big sacrifice at first, but when you stop to consider it, moving home to save on rent can net you a tidy little profit. Whether you're staying for two or five years, and provided you're socking away your rent check each month because your parents are letting you crash rent-free, here's a breakdown of the kind of nest egg you can expect to build.

Monthly Rent: $1,000
Duration at Home: 1 year
Total Savings: $12,000

Monthly Rent: $1,000
Duration at Home: 2 years
Total Savings: $24,000

Monthly Rent: $1,000
Duration at Home: 3 years
Total Savings: $36,000

Monthly Rent: $1,000
Duration at Home: 4 years
Total Savings: $48,000

Provided you invest your money wisely, the "total savings" could be much higher due to interest and stock returns.

SCHOOL OF HARD KNOCKS

Stan's story, while surprising to some, is hardly unique. Rising school loans and tuition hikes play a huge role in the evolution of the boomerang culture. According to the Department of Education in 1980, federal Pell grants accounted for about 77 percent of the cost of a four-year institution. Today, that number has slid to a paltry 40 percent, and getting one of these grants is tougher than ever. With the new changes in the eligibility requirements made by the Department of Education, about 84,000 incoming students will be excluded from the program entirely. With Pell grants falling faster than Britney Spears's record sales and universities raising tuition fees due to a lack of state and federal support, many have to work overtime to make ends meet.

In the past, a high-school diploma was enough to land a middle-class income and lifestyle. Your dad or granddad graduated from high school, landed a job at the local steel mill, and was able to provide for a family of three. These days, a high school degree won't get you much. According to the U.S. Census Bureau, college graduates earned 80 percent more than people with only a high school diploma. So in order to match the standard of living enjoyed by our parents, we have no choice but to buckle down and get an advanced four-year degree.

On top of being virtually mandatory, a college degree now takes longer than ever to acquire. While most students used to breeze through the curriculum in a four-year period, that time frame has gotten considerably longer. On average, only one-third of students who enter four-year colleges straight from high school graduate on time. With so many students transferring schools, switching majors, and taking time off to work, many experts have established six years as the new, more realistic graduation timeline.

Tempting as it is for us to dawdle on campus for five years or more, we rarely acknowledge the damage it's doing to our bank account until it is too late. After six years of kicking and screaming, most of us will be saddled with an average school loan of $18,000.

For many students, paying off their school loan on an entry-level salary is a formidable feat. After the monthly installment is paid, the rent handed in, and the bills mailed, there's just not enough money left to go around. So is it any wonder that when faced with the prospect of paying off their school debt and living on our own, many of us are opting to return home in droves?

DEBT-FREE BY 60

With escalating school loans, credit card companies aggressively marketing on campuses across the country, and almost no education available on the topic of credit, the financial picture for many young adults is bleak at best. It's gotten to the point where experts are calling us "Generation D" (for debt) or "Generation B" (for bankrupt). And with more than 615,000 people age 35 and under filing for bankruptcy in 2000 (according to a Harvard Law School study), it may be time to admit that we may indeed have a problem managing our money.

Caught up in a highly consumptive culture where the message is to "charge now, pay later," many young adults are finding themselves knee-deep in debt before they've even held down their first full-time job. According to a Nellie May study published in 2002, over 83 percent of college undergraduates carried credit cards; the average debt for graduating seniors is now estimated at around $3,000.

But young people aren't spending just on late-night pizza fests and high-tech gadgets, either. With the rise in tuition fees and less financial aid to go around, many college students are using credit cards to pay for their education. Not a good idea, of course, since the interest on school loans is considerably lower than that offered by credit-card companies.

For the most part, young adults are in the dark about bad credit habits. They'll max out one card only to apply for a new one or pay off the minimum of one card by charging it to another. Caught up in a vicious spiral of spending and debt, many twenty- and thirtysomethings are finding that the only way to get out of the cycle is to take cover at home while paying off their balance.

Cedit Cards: Why the House Always Wins

Much like lavish Las Vegas casinos, credit-card companies seem warm and fuzzy when they're trying to get you hooked. They'll offer you T-shirts, free flyer miles, bonus points at your favorite shops. But once your back is against the wall and you're down for a cool ten grand, they're anything but friendly. Of course, that's not to say that credit-card companies are evil. No, greed and rampant consumption are the true culprits here. Remember free will? Only you can decide if you're going to let the plastic make you or break you. These quick facts may help you come to your senses.

- If you pay just the minimum each month, it will take 30 years to settle a $2,000 credit card balance.
- According to a Quicken survey, almost 71 percent of college students carry debt on their credit card.
- In the 1970s, young adults/college students could not obtain credit cards without a cosigner or letter of employment.
- Today, kids as young as 13 are being targeted by credit-card companies.
- One out of ten undergraduates has credit-card debt greater than $7,000.

DELAYING THE INEVITABLE

With all the goalposts of adulthood—housing, economic independence, employment, completion of education—getting harder and harder to achieve, it's not surprising that so many of us are choosing to turn back instead of run ahead.

Adolescence used to be defined as a time of personal struggle for identity that ended with the choice of a career and a spouse. Among the markers on the chronological road to adulthood: Get a job at 18 or 22. Get married between 18 and 23. Become a responsible adult. Have kids. Today's generation questions such handy definitions. Boomerangers ask, "Isn't making decisions for yourself a vital part of being a responsible adult? How is blindly trying to live up to society's expectations indicative of adulthood?"

The current generation is living in a time of shifting realities and downgraded expectations. Stripped of the sense of entitlement that characterized our younger years—that feeling that the world owes us a better lifestyle than our parents enjoyed—many boomerangers now believe that it's best to go with the flow and not push too hard or expect too much when forging a personal or professional future.

> In today's rigorous economy and dynamically changing world it becomes difficult for many recent graduates to acclimate and adjust to a new environment in which they must support themselves. With this life change often comes anxiety, confusion, and an overall lack of direction. I for one didn't know what I was going to do with my life or what was being offered in the employment world. Going home gave me a haven to get my life together and make decisions as to which paths I would take.
>
> —Steve, 23, Philadelphia, PA

The twenties are increasingly becoming a time to explore, experiment, and self-actualize. With many of our parents wishing that they could have benefited from a similar pressure-free zone in which to explore career options, relationships, and identities, they are more than willing to support us financially and emotionally as we go through one transition after another.

"I call it the self-focus age. It's the one time in life where you can decide for yourself how to live, without having to compromise or get someone else's permission. The focus is on your own self-development," explains Jeffrey J. Arnett, a professor of human development at the University of Maryland and the author of *Emerging Adulthood: The Winding Road from the Late Teens through the Twenties.*

If adolescence is defined as the time between puberty and being saddled with responsibility for other people, then maybe 30 really is the new 20, as so many recent polls and social scientists have expressed. Take the "Coming of Age in the 21st Century" study conducted by the University of Chicago's National Opinion Research Center (NORC): When asked at what age someone becomes a full-fledged adult, most people answered 26. But the truth is that even by the age of 30, most of us have yet to pass through the five major transitions of adulthood:

1. Finishing school
2. Leaving the family home
3. Establishing financial independence
4. Starting a family of one's own

According to one study conducted in 2000, only 46 percent of women and 31 percent of men have successfully achieved all the above by age 30. The truth is, many boomerangers don't really begin to understand the reasons behind getting married, having children, and throwing themselves headlong into a career until much later. The master plan of job-spouse-kids seems robbed of personal meaning, abstract, far-removed and sometimes even undesirable. As a result, many boomerangers live out the Peter Pan existence, making the idea of "extended adolescence" an all-too-popular reality.

Now I think the whole thing about being an adult is twisted. Their idea of a normal life is taking a job you hate, saving money just so you can go on vacation. My parents may not think I'm an adult because I don't have a stupid desk job so I can be

bored, miserable, and depressed and be able to buy a sweater
at the end of each week. But who cares?

—Heidi, 27, Newport, RI

These new expectations for the onset of adulthood have had a
profound effect on the number of young adults who bid their over-
priced, modestly priced, even dirt-cheap apartments farewell when
the going gets tough. Living with Mom and Dad in return for
peace of mind may not seem like such a bad deal, especially at a
time when the boundaries between childhood and adulthood are
becoming progressively more blurred.

Kiddie Culture

Don't want to grow up, do
you? Well, who does? The
Concise Oxford Dictionary even has a definition for this phenomenon:
"Adultescent: a middle-aged person whose clothes, interests and activities are typically associated with youth culture." With so many options
for embracing our inner brat, it's no wonder we're trying to stave off
adulthood a little longer. Here are some signs of our ever-growing regression nation:

- The cross-generational appeal of Harry Potter movies and books
- Hello Kitty mugs and calendars littering our office spaces
- Adult candy stores with oversized jelly pretzels and cotton candy
  sticks opening across the nation
- Playstation's popularity with the late twenties set
- Mattel's launch of a Barbie line of clothes, accessories, and per-
  fume for adult women
- Cars being packaged as Tonka-like mini-trucks for young buyers
- High-tech toys like iPods and BlackBerries marketed to grown-up
  boys and girls
- The revival of Strawberry Shortcake products, with the marketing
  slogan "Who knew you and your daughter would have the same best
  friend?"

BAIT-AND-SWITCH

Faced with an enormous debt load upon graduation, many of us are
in no position to pick and choose when it comes to accepting a job

right out of college. In fact, most recent graduates report having to take the first job offered. Fortunately, today's young adults are finding that they can safely take a leap into a new, more satisfying career path without having to toil in unfulfilling occupations.

In these days of corporate mergers, mass layoffs, and constant reorganizations, company loyalty has gone the way of the dinosaur. The idea of having one job your entire life is pretty far-fetched. In fact, according to the Bureau of Labor Statistics, we're moving through jobs with lightning speed, with the average person holding down 9.2 jobs between ages 18 and 34.

While most employers used to view job hoppers as disloyal employees with commitment issues, the stigma of playing career leapfrog has decreased over the years. Today, some corporations even consider these people to be proactive challenge seekers and look down at candidates who stay at entry-level jobs for too long. In a 2000 JobTrak survey, 27 percent of recent graduates expected to leave their first job after one year, and only 22 percent thought they would stay longer than three years.

I had originally gone to film school and planned to become the next big female director. So first there was the two-year stint at the movie production studio. When that didn't work out as planned, I switched to new media and spent three years working at corporate websites. It was fun for a while, but I realized I could never be happy working at a large company. I finally decided to go off on my own and start a career as a freelance writer. I could never do that if I hadn't decided to move home with my parents for six months. It takes time to build your resume and portfolio. Who knows? I'll probably end up staying even longer. But what's the alternative, staying in a job I hate or am bored with just because I'm scared to move back home?
—Stacy, 25, Akron, OH

No doubt about it, the twenties are all about staying fluid. Everything is constantly shifting, including friends, career goals, and living arrangements. There's just no telling where one will end up from year to year. Young adults who are bored, frustrated, or uninspired by their jobs are grateful for the chance to quit sooner rather than later. And if moving home to their parents will allow them to find more fulfilling work, then that's a compromise many of them are more than willing to make.

OLD-WORLD VALUES

Greeks, Italians, Asians, Russians . . . many of them are living in a three-generation household—and liking it. As more immigrants pour onto our shores, we're seeing a major overhaul of the traditional family unit. While Westerners tend to raise children to be more independent and self-sufficient, other cultures still place a greater premium on cooperation and communal living. And with this influence from our friendly newcomers, the strictly American notion of "be all you can be, so long as you don't do it in my house" value system has undergone a dramatic shift.

> Culturally, both my parents are Peruvian. It's common to move out when you are married, but before then it doesn't really make any sense and really isn't accepted. My parents live close to the city and I have always worked in or around the city, so financially it didn't seem like it made sense to move out until I was married. I think it's my own decision, not because I can't afford living on my own, but I feel like I am making a wise and responsible decision and in the long run I will be more successful than my friends. My parents have always respected the fact that I've decided to stay and save money and that I honor our culture and their wishes.
>
> —Mary, 30, San Diego, CA

The common conception is that the majority of ethnic families are from lower income brackets and need to live together in order to make ends meet. And while that is sometimes the case, it's hardly the whole story. Statistics show that many of these families aren't living together strictly out of necessity. Young adults from middle-class immigrant families choose to stay home for many other reasons, including family intimacy and emotional support. It's a cultural value that they're not so quick to toss aside as soon as they land on U.S. soil.

I was happy to be back with my family after a few years away from them. I was living with my mother, father, my two brothers, my sister. The relationships definitely changed. My family is very close and for me to be there is good because I felt really energized by that. I saw what's more important in life—having a family and being close. I appreciate the values they have and the respect they show each other. My aunts who moved away from the family are very different from us. They have both been divorced. I feel very lucky that my parents are still together for 30 years. My parents care for me, do stuff for me, and help me when I need it. You have their love and their care, and you appreciate what you have.

—Sandra, 29, Valley Stream, NY

BREAKING UP IS HARD TO DO

We've all heard the little ditty about Jack and Diane, the sweethearts who married right out of high school. And while that used be the norm, the idea of getting married in our early twenties seems completely alien to many of us. If jumping from one job to another is any indication of our ability to commit, then it's not at all surprising to find out that our personal relationships are often equally if not more precarious. Many young adults view their twenties as a time to figure out what they want once they're ready to get married. Shacking up, dating, playing the field—it's all part of finding out who we are. And with marriage being postponed longer and longer, it's not surprising that we find ourselves creating bonds with our existing families rather than forging new ones.

With so many of us getting on and off the relationship roller

I Do and I Don't   The U.S. Census Bureau's marriage statistics show that the boomerang generation is waiting longer than any other to settle down and start families. Between 1970 and 2000 the average age at first marriage for women increased from 20.8 to 25.1. For men, it rose from 23.2 to 26.8 years.

coaster, it's not surprising to find many boomerangers returning home after a particularly bumpy ride. While the exes left in our wake may not have been "the ones," the feelings of loss and emotional isolation that often follow are still just as poignant and painful. The comfort of home never seems so appealing as when we're feeling down for the count and incapable of picking ourselves up. And spending some time with our parents is often just the antidote we need to mend our broken hearts.

> I was living with my boyfriend in Manhattan the summer before my last semester in college and I decided to end the relationship after I graduated instead of moving back in with him after school. I felt a little defeated, both because my three-year relationship didn't work out and because I had to move home. It was a really big blow. I also felt very comforted to be around my family for support. I think they were happy that I wasn't staying with that particular guy. My parents have always been clear that my brother and I are welcome in their home no matter what happens.
>
> —Dana, 26, Ballston Lake, NY

FRIENDS FOR LIFE

Whether it was *The Breakfast Club* motto of "never trust anyone over 30," James Dean in *Rebel Without a Cause*, or the beats Jazzy Jeff & the Fresh Prince laid down in "Parents Just Don't Understand," the tension between old and new generations has been well documented. And for good reason. It used to be that parents and teenagers went together like oil and water. We expected to fight over every little issue, and vehemently guarded our turf with signs reading "Keep Out" and "Parent-Free Zone."

Not that we could be blamed, of course. The parents of yesteryear didn't understand our music, our clothes, or our choices. Worst of all, many of them didn't care to. The idea of being friends with their kids just wasn't that important. But that's all in the past.

For many boomerangers, the big question today isn't whether you can afford to live apart from your parents, but whether you would even want to.

My mom and I have pretty much everything in common. We both like disaster flicks, eating sushi with our hands, going to swap meets, and conspiracy theories. It's like having a best friend and parent all wrapped up in one. Funny thing is we weren't even that close all through high school or college. When I moved back home from Boston, after being laid off from a magazine, I lost touch with a lot of my old friends from the city. Luckily, my mom and I got really close, really fast. I never expected that I would enjoy being with her so much.

—Trista, 23, Portland, ME

It's not just people in their twenties and thirties who are embracing the youth culture. It's our parents, too! Go into any shopping mall across the country, and it's like a Stepford parent convention. Parents are dressing, talking, and even walking like us. Let's face it, many parents have become cool. They understand our need for privacy, our need to take risks, and our need to find ourselves. In fact, most of them understand so well that they find themselves living vicariously through us as we zip from one adventure to the next.

Paradoxically, the more freedom our parents gave us in the past, the more likely we'll be to cling to their apron strings. When there's no one or nothing to rebel against, most young adults find their parents to be more than adequate companions.

One Big Happy Family While they're not all cut from the same cool cloth, today's parents have a much better idea of what we're going through. It's okay to admit you actually like your parents. Judging by these statistics from the Mood of America Youth Survey, there's many more where you came from.

⟶ In 1974, about 50 percent of young people had no serious problems with parents.
⟶ In 1983, about 74 percent had no serious problems with their parents.
⟶ In 1996, about 94 percent of teenagers were very happy or fairly happy with one or both parents.

With the war on terror, the poor economy, and the general sense of fear and insecurity sweeping the globe, home has become the last safe haven for many young people looking for a little stability. But sometimes it's not fear or economic hardships that are driving us home so much as a general desire to be around those we love most. And with parents providing so much breathing room and the freedom to be ourselves, many boomerangers are suddenly finding that home has truly become the one place where the heart is—or, at the very least, the one place with free cable.

2

READY, SET, BOOMERANG!

The last thing I wanted was to end up like my 28-year-old brother, you know, with my backside permanently glued to the couch and my mom still doing my laundry. So after graduating, I set out for Los Angeles to become a talent agent. I was living in a filthy apartment with three other people I didn't know very well. My room was more a walk-in closet than an actual bedroom, and we shared one bathroom between the four of us. For a while I paid my dues at one of the biggest talent agencies, working for a prick boss who surfed porn sites all day. But I was barely making enough money to cover my rent.

It was gradual, but eventually I spiraled into total misery. One minute I would pack all my stuff and be ready to go home. And then I would unpack, feeling like the biggest loser in the world for even considering giving up. I spent one painful year in limbo as I weighed all the pros and cons. I was just waiting for some sign to make my decision easier. Finally, I threw in the towel. I was running out of money and needed to make a decision— fast! I decided to move back home to Pittsburgh and get my life together.

—Julie, 29, Pittsburgh, PA

Whether you're still weighing the pros and cons of boomeranging or have already taken the plunge, you're probably grappling with some difficult questions. Making the decision to move back home is probably one of the toughest you'll ever make. Let's face it: With everything you would be gaining (cheap/rent-free living, home-cooked meals, full-service laundry, the companionship of your nearest and dearest), you'd also be giving up a lot, including your privacy, a certain amount of autonomy, and the ability to choose your own brand of toilet paper.

As you ponder your options, millions of contradictory thoughts will be running through your head. There's your parents to consider (do they even want me around?), the fear of losing friends (will I spend every Friday night watching *Touched by an Angel* reruns?), and the constant nagging fear that once you move home, you'll get sucked into a morass of sloth and procrastination. For every solid reason you have for living with your parents, you probably have another equally good one for staying far, far away.

Give yourself a little credit. In no way does being on the fence about this issue make you indecisive or flaky. On the contrary, by seriously considering cohabitating with the 'rents, you're joining the ranks of millions of young people who are bucking tradition and social expectation in an effort to figure out what's right for them. If you weren't a little confused, then you'd have real reason to worry.

Let's just stop to consider the fact that much of our twenties and thirties is spent in a sea of deep confusion and self-analysis, and their inevitable offspring—total paralysis. Is it any surprise that we feel angsty and insecure? As a group, we tend to agonize over every little thing, fearing that one wrong move will result in a lifetime of bad habits, unforeseen consequences, and perpetual regrets: If I order the Whopper instead of the chicken salad, will my children grow up to be fast-food junkies and video game addicts? If I don't ask for a raise in six months, will I become a low-paid, staple-counting pushover? If I move back home, will I be destined to live with my mother and her three Siamese cats forever?

While some questions just lead to more questions, not asking them at all is even more dangerous. Doing nothing is a choice in itself. If you choose to ignore the reality of your finances, your mounting debt, or your lack of life direction just because you're terrified of moving back home, you'll have a new reality to deal with that may be even more unpleasant.

After all, what's the alternative? Denial? While it may seem that all your freewheeling friends who swear they'd never move home have it all figured out, the reality may be much grimmer.

Take Rusty, a 28-year-old from New York. On the surface, his life seemed to be the picture of overachieving bliss. After attending New York University School of Law, getting a high-six-figure job at a prestigious law firm, and plunking down his signing bonus on a cool SoHo loft, he was all set for a life of ease and prosperity in New York City. After years of late-night cramming sessions and deferring gratification, Rusty felt entitled to let loose and live the high life. He started going out excessively and blowing through cash as quickly as he made it. Pretty soon, his financial negligence had seeped into his professional life. Coming in late, avoiding responsibility, and acting belligerent with his coworkers had become his standard MO. On the rare occasions when Rusty did show up on time, his attitude was lousy. After only nine months on the job, he was unceremoniously fired.

With all those years in law school behind him, all he had to show for himself was a huge mortgage, a $100,000 loan, and few job prospects. His mother, a divorcée living in Rochester, New York, begged him to move home and save up enough money to pay off his debts. But her appeal fell on deaf ears. He refused to confront his mounting debt or curb his spending, shelling out cash for luxuries like electronics, VIP bottle service at the latest hot spots, and expensive dinners for his dates. After a few more months, Rusty hit rock-bottom. He defaulted on his mortgage and was being hounded by creditors. He was forced to sell the loft for much less than the original purchase price and moved back to the suburbs to live with his mother. A year later he was lucky enough to find work at a smaller law firm close to home, but his salary wasn't enough to move out on. Rusty figures he has six more years at home in order to pay off his debts. But even if he did have the money to rent his own apartment, his credit is so bad he's worried that no landlord will approve his application.

The truth is that nothing lasts forever—neither your triumphs nor what you perceive as your failures. Whether you're already boomeranged or still mulling it over, you'll find that all the roads you thought were closed to you will still be very much wide open. So why not consider moving back home as an opportunity? There's absolutely no reason why you can't still start that small business, go back to school to learn fashion design, or master some investment strategies and become financially solvent. Whatever your fears, don't let them get the best of you. This is just another stage in your life, with its own share of upsides and potential downfalls.

That's why this chapter is so important. The decision to move back home should be made without panic, self-recrimination, or fear that you'll never become an independent adult. This chapter will help you figure out whether the move makes sense for you, come to grips with all the possible ramifications, and feel good about your decision—whatever it may be. You'll also find a "moving in" action plan that will help you tie up loose ends and make an easier transition home.

And even if you've already jumped over the threshold with both feet, it would be in your best interest to review this section. It's never too late to take a good hard look at your situation and deal with issues that have yet to be resolved.

THE ADULT THING TO DO

Art school led to a few jobs in graphic design, but nothing stable or permanent. I've always wanted to sculpt, but I didn't know if this was realistic. My parents are pretty well off, so I thought I could fall back on them if I needed help. But when they offered me $10,000 to help me settle into my new life, I couldn't go through with it. I saw a lot of my friends struggling, and I felt like such a hypocrite. I couldn't be like, "Look how well I'm doing, but my parents are picking up the tab." Believe me, I was very tempted to take it and run. Ultimately, I decide to move back home. It might not have been a decision that made sense to my friends, or even my parents for that matter, but knowing I was saving my own money gave me a lot of confidence. Pretty soon, I was able to get a few of my pieces into an art gallery and things have been picking up since then. I don't know if I'm going to be able to support myself doing what I do, but I'm more optimistic than ever.

—Carl, 26, Santa Fe, NM

The decision to rebound home is often viewed as a sign of immaturity; that we, the boomerangers, are somehow less capable and evolved when we choose to head home. It's only natural to wonder how returning to our old rooms—stuffed toys, sports trophies, and all—could actually turn out to be the adult thing to do.

While it may not seem terribly mature, it's often better than the alternative. With so many young adults living on their own but above their means, hitting up their parents for yet another cash advance, and going into debt to prove how independent they are, defining what it means to be an adult is tougher than ever. After all, shouldn't adulthood be measured by how well someone functions in the real world instead of by where they live? Would it help you to know that many of your so-called "independent" peers are probably more reliant on their parents than they've led you to believe? In fact, according to the Institute for Social Research, 34 percent of all 18- to 34-year-olds (including those who live on their own) receive cash from their parents. So you see? Moving back home doesn't mean forsaking your autonomy—it just means that you're less likely to hit up Mom and Dad for cash. Depending on your approach, you can be as independent, if not more, at home than those living solo.

All things considered, boomeranging is a much tougher choice. While you can still seem like an adult when you're living in the apartment Mom and Dad paid for, living at home makes it virtually impossible to save face. It's all too easy to get bogged down by what everyone will think of you. By confronting your own pared down circumstances head-on and defying convention, you have actually shown yourself to be *more* of an adult. The ability to make decisions based on your fiscal reality and not some idealized picture of where you should be is what truly separates the kids from the grown-ups.

Compromise is an integral part of being an adult. If you opt to go back to grad school, you'll need to trim back your lifestyle. If you decide to marry and have a family, you'll need to stop playing the field. If you want to succeed at a nine-to-five job, you'll have to say good-bye to staying up and partying all night. It's just a matter of deciding what your priorities are and sticking to them.

NO JOB, NO APARTMENT, NO LIFE–NO PROBLEM!

During the boom of the late 1990s, it made perfect sense to move out on our own, chase the mirage of dot-com riches, and forge urban tribes with our like-minded cappuccino-sipping peers. With a boundless enthusiasm in our step, we forged ahead, not even stopping to look back at the nervous but proud expressions on our friends' and family's faces. Our contagious optimism was enough to carry us through the hard times and allowed us to squelch our fears as we looked forward to a brighter future. We hoped that the job as an administrative assistant would turn into a corner office, the starter apartment we shared with three friends would turn into a luxury one-bedroom pad overlooking the river, and that our college debt would magically pay itself off. And while some of those things did happen to our next-door neighbors, our third cousin on our Mom's side, or maybe even our best friend, they have yet to happen to us.

Today's economic climate brings with it a wealth of new, less

Taking the Plunge: Are You Ready to Boomerang?

Readiness is a state of mind. While you may never be fully ready to move back home, you may be more prepared than you think. Before you set your sails for the comfy shores of home, take this quiz to help you decide. Of course, no quiz or formula (however scientifically sound) will be able to make this decision for you. So in the end, you'll have to listen to your gut before making the final call.

1. Your savings account has a balance of $500 or less—and it's plummeting fast!　　　　　　　　　　　　　　　　True / False

2. You're pretty confident you'll be able to find part- or full-time work in your family hometown　　　　　　　　　　　　True / False

3. You have a close group of friends who'll be there for you when you move home.　　　　　　　　　　　　　　　　True / False

4. You wake up in a sweat from nightmares of credit card and school loan hell at least once a week.　　　　　　　　　True / False

5. You have big goals for the future (buying a house, saving for retirement, attending graduate school, starting a small business), but you have no idea how you will accomplish these things living on your own.

True / False

6. You try to visit your parents at least once a month, and can usually spend a day with them without any major fights breaking out.

True / False

7. You're paying an astronomical amount of rent for a room the size of your parents' bathroom.   True / False

8. Your parents generally respect your decisions and support you in achieving your goals.   True / False

9. You've been hit hard by a series of harsh life events and need time out to regroup.   True / False

10. You're burnt-out and unmotivated at your current job, and are seriously considering a career change.   True / False

11. You view the move home as a temporary event until you can figure out your next step.   True / False

SCORING

7–11 TRUES: If you answered True to more than seven of the questions above, you may be a prime candidate for boomeranging. You have a good idea of what brought you to this point and will most likely be able to make a smooth transition home.

4–6 TRUES: While you're probably not ready to call it quits yet, you would benefit from seriously considering boomeranging.

1–3 TRUES: Whoa! Aren't you being a bit hasty? Okay, so maybe not everything in your life is going as planned, but are you really ready to take the next step?

exciting considerations. Simply put, the playing field has changed. No longer do we expect to make our millions by age 30 and retire by the time we turn 40. Okay, maybe we didn't expect to do all that. But even if we hoped to simply match the comfortable lifestyles of our parents, it's getting harder and harder to do even that. With housing prices soaring through the roof, unemployment rampant, college debt rising, and the cost of health care going sky-high, we should be so lucky as our middle-class parents.

When we left adolescence behind, we thought it was for good. So when the reality turned out to be less than ideal, as our struggles multiplied and our hopes began to dwindle, we were forced to confront a new option, one that we may never have expected, wanted, or even brought ourselves to think about.

SO MANY BOOMERANGERS

Before we continue, give yourself some credit for taking time to ponder what is bound to become the most interesting and unpredictable stage of your life. It's important to be aware that since not all boomerangers are created equal, each of you will have a dramatically different experience living at home. Consider all the possible scenarios:

- Men vs. women boomerangers
- Boomerangers moving into tiny cramped houses vs. *MTV Cribs*–like penthouses.
- People moving home in their early twenties, late twenties, thirties, and even forties.
- Moving in with parents in the city, or moving to remote locations with a population of 2,000.
- Returning to a two-parent home, or one where parents have divorced and is now a single-parent household.

Since the possibilities are endless, you'd be well advised to consider your situation before coming to a firm decision. And while you won't find specific advice for dealing with each scenario until later in the book, you will find a quick primer that will get you on your way to making a decision.

But don't forget: No decision is ever final. If you move home and decide you hate it, you can always pack your bags and hightail it out of there. After all, it's your life and you have the prerogative to change your mind.

I was growing more and more overwhelmed with living in New York City. Being from a small city where I already knew everyone, I always felt a little bit out of place. I'd been struggling financially in the big city for about one and a half years and thought that it would all be magically better if I moved back home to Peekskill. I got a job in my hometown and moved in with Mom and Dad. I thought I was going to have the life I wanted. Money in the bank, a car, a steady and reliable job, my old friends. I was homesick and wanted things to go back the way they used to be. But in a matter of days, I realized it wasn't what I really wanted. After two weeks, I was going crazy. When I told my parents I was moving out again, they were more than a little mad at me. But in the end, I had to do what I did. It made me realize how much I really liked living on my own.

—Kelly, 27, Saratoga Springs, NY

Whatever boat you find yourself in, you'll recognize yourself in the descriptions below. Most important, you'll realize just how many of you are out there. Just knowing that there are others like you can significantly eliminate the anxiety associated with this little-talked-about but all-too-prevalent phenomenon.

MOMMA'S BOYS VERSUS GIRLS

It may surprise some of you to find out that more men are boomeranging than women. According to the latest census data, 64 percent of men aged 20 to 24 live at home, with only 52 percent of women in that age bracket doing the same.

Of course, Italian bachelors, or "Mamones," have been doing it for years. Their mothers do everything for them, including ironing their shirts and cutting their steak. But when did it start happening so much here on American soil? Most of us assume that if a guy lives at home with his parents, he's got a major glitch somewhere. Images of Norman Bates in *Psycho* flash through our minds—talk about the dangers of never leaving home! But even with all these stereotypes of momma's boys and psycho stalkers, the numbers don't lie: Men are moving home in droves.

Of course, part of the reason for the gender discrepancy is

that women still tend to get married earlier. With the median age of marrying women at 25 and men at 28, one reason that men often choose to postpone starting new families is because they're still residing with their old ones.

And why wouldn't they? No matter how unfair it seems, parents are still more lenient when it comes to setting rules for their sons than for their daughters. So with the Cinderella treatment being alive and well, it's no wonder young women are less likely to stick around. Take a look at some of the evidence:

Men	Women
More social freedom, like going out and spending nights at friends' houses	Less social freedom
Parents expect male boomerangers to do fewer chores	Parents expect female boomerangers to do more chores
More opportunity for bringing home dates and significant others.	Less opportunity for bringing home dates and significant others

So what does all this mean for you? Well, for the men out there, you're probably cheering, expecting to come home to a more civilized version of *Animal House*. But even with all the extra privileges and freedoms, brace yourself for the reality that it will be harder to find dates while living at home. While some of you wouldn't think twice about getting busy in the bedroom next to your parents', others will find it extremely disturbing.

For the women out there, don't be put off by what seems to be an unreasonable double standard. Many women living at home report having thriving social lives, with parents being understanding of their need to stay active on the dating scene. And while Mom and Dad may scoff at the idea of you gallivanting all over town, good communication should help them realize that you're entitled to many of the same privileges you had while living on your own.

STEP INTO THE AGE GAP

Think age is just a number? Think again. When it comes to moving back home, it can make a huge difference.

Early Twenties

If you're moving home in your early twenties, chances are you're probably not overly traumatized by the prospect. With over 60 percent of recent college grads reporting having to return home for at least six months (according to Monster TRAK), you'll probably have plenty of friends to commiserate with. With entry-level jobs paying as little as they do, no one really expects you to support yourself on that pittance. Not only that, since unemployment is so high, it's a good chance you're probably still looking for your first job or are even forced to take a nonpaying internship while you gain the necessary experience. If all else fails, recent college grads could always console themselves with the idea that their situation is only temporary. After all, you have your whole life ahead of you, and your optimism should help you weather the storm. It's not like you'll ever come home again—at least, that's what you keep telling yourself.

With almost 60 percent of American 22- to 24-year-olds currently living at home, parents obviously are much more likely to welcome their young graduates back into the family fold. Most will treat your return as a one-time event, and will savor what they think is their last moment of bonding before you strike out on your own. If they only knew! If statistics hold true, many of you will rebound home again at some point in your twenties or thirties. And some of you may get so comfy at home that you find leaving more difficult than anticipated. While your folks may have been okay with your arrival the first time around, researchers Audra W. Clemens and Leland J. Axelson report parents' patience wearing thin with each subsequent return and indefinitely postponed departure.

Mid to Late Twenties

For those of you in your mid to late twenties, the situation may be a bit trickier. By now, you've probably spent a considerable amount of time doing your own thing. You've either rented an apartment, cohabitated with roommates, or lived with a significant other. But with over 30 percent of people aged 25 to 29 moving home, rest assured you're not alone.

Having been left to your own devices, it may be harder for you to adjust to your new living circumstances than your younger peers. Expectations of where you "should," "could," and "would" be, coupled with pressure from your friends and family to get on with your life, can also complicate the matter, making your time at home more anxiety-ridden. Of course, it's all a matter of how you look at it. Your experience can be as stressful or rewarding as you make it. (More on that in Chapter 8.)

Thirties and Forties

Still, for those in their mid to late twenties who think they have it rough, consider what it's like to move home in your thirties or even your forties. With one in four 30- to 34-year-olds said to be boomerangers, there are probably more out there than you think. By this point, most of you have probably had more than a few experiences under your belt. Some of you would even consider yourselves full-fledged adults. While unemployment and financial debt still rank high on the list of reasons to move home, many people in their thirties and forties also return because of concern for parents living on their own.

I never thought that at this age I'd be at home at the age of 40. But at the same time, I'm able to save lots of money, as well as help my mom out financially and around the house. So I'm torn sometimes between loving and hating it. But it's more mature to realize that on my salary, which is not bad but not great, either, it's better to live at home than just work to pay the rent and not have money for other things. Plus, at this point in time, I wouldn't want to leave my mom on her own. She's in perfect

health and we do go out to movies, dinner, and even travel together. We have similar tastes in many things so I'm glad I'm
old enough now to appreciate her friendship and advice when I
need it.

—Tyler, 40, New York, NY

There's no way around it: The older you get, the greater the
stigma of moving home. Whereas most Generation Ys view the
move home as temporary and welcoming, Generation Xers are
often resentful and distressed about the situation, seeing it as an indicator of failure rather than just another life passage. Whatever
your age, there's no denying the fact that moving back home is a
major transition. It's important to remember that life doesn't always move from point A to point Z in a seamless line, and the many
detours, pauses, and stops along the way are just as important as the
final destination.

GLOBAL WARNING

Whether you're planning to have a big fat Greek, Italian, or Indian
wedding, your family's ethnicity and culture will play a huge role in
how you handle the transition. Those of you born into Latino or
Russian families have probably lived in a home with grandparents
and are used to the idea of cohabitation with elderly members of
the family. Having been raised with this cultural expectation,
you've probably have had more time to get acclimated to the idea
of living with parents. It's not so much a matter of being treated
differently when you get there—although there will be some
marked differences depending on your background—but more a
matter of being adequately forewarned.

Being Greek-American, I was always expected to move home
after graduation. Most of my friends thought that living with my
parents meant that I was going to be doing nothing, that I
would spend my days eating souvlaki while waiting for a hus-
band to show up on my doorstep. They don't understand. Just
because my parents want me at home doesn't mean I'm not expected to contribute. I have a full-time job and pay rent. I even
help babysit my cousins, which is a lot more than I can say for

some of my friends living with their families. It's not about mooching off my parents. It's about sharing my life with people I love most.

—Christa, 29, Downers Grove, IL

Around the World If you think 18 million boomerangers in the United States is a large number, consider these staggering stats of 20- to 34-year-olds living at home:

- In the UK, 12.2 million live with parents.
- In France, 16.6 million live at home.
- In Germany, 12.3 million have boomeranged.
- In Japan, 27 million are homebounders.

MOM. DAD. WE'RE HOME!

Despite the fact that about 90 percent of boomerangers are single with no dependents, that still leaves plenty of single parents and married couples coming home to roost with parents. Whether you're moving home single with child or as part of a couple, you'll need to consider every contingency.

Parents Living with Parents

If you're newly divorced or happily married, parents moving in with parents should realize that the presence of children will be a considerable drain on the family's resources. One study by researchers William Aquilino and Khalil Supple found that while most parents were satisfied with one boomeranger at home, having grandchildren in the house significantly decreased that comfort level.

Moving in and expecting parents to babysit, clean up, and chase after your tots is asking for trouble. Not only that, many boomerangers report having boundary issues when it comes to child-rearing. You and your mom may have very different ideas about how much TV the kids should watch and when they should go to sleep. It's a question of who exactly is raising whom.

Still, that's not to say that all families are completely unsatisfied with this kind of living arrangement. Some parents will be overjoyed at the prospect of spending time with their grandkids. But by being prepared to keep up your end of the bargain—making sure your kid(s) behave, discussing boundaries early on, and reimbursing your parents for any extra expenses that may creep up—you'll have a better chance of maintaining household harmony.

Three's a Crowd

For those of you without kids but with a spouse in tow, be ready to deal with your own share of gripes (this could be a book in itself). Today, many newlyweds are choosing to move in with one set of in-laws in order to save for a house or recover from a financial blow. While it's not an uncommon scenario, it does come with its own share of difficulties.

Couples living with in-laws may find their time alone significantly reduced and may feel estranged from each other. The wife or hubbie may also experience compatibility issues with the parents, which could put a strain on the marriage as well. The key to success will be to outline all the potential problems and to establish a space that is uniquely your own. Marriage is tough enough when it's just the two of you, but when the in-laws get involved, prepare to do some serious damage control.

> My husband, Andy, and I moved into my family's home after he lost his job due to a disability. My salary as a paralegal wasn't enough to tide us over, and rental prices had gone up since we moved into the area four years ago. At first, we were horrified by the idea of losing our privacy and space. I don't think my parents were thrilled, either. But we explained it would only be temporary, until Dave got his settlement from the company. It was tough for a while. My husband and my mother butted heads a lot. She resented him for always being around the house, and thought he should have been taking his physical therapy more seriously. By the time the year was up and our settlement came through, I was ecstatic to be out of there. None of us was prepared for how difficult living together would be.
>
> —Delia, 32, Gainesville, FL

BOOMERANGNATION

37

RICH DAD, POOR DAD

Whether you're a Vanderbilt or a Snodgrass, the size of your family home can make a huge difference in your time at home.

Rich Dad

Those of you moving back into sprawling mansions with an entire east wing to call your very own will never know the pain of having to share a room in a cramped house. Of course, most people with huge estates are likely to have trust funds to match and will usually opt to spend them on a place of their own. But even if that's not an option, consider yourself lucky to have room to breathe. You will be able to come and go as you please (did someone say guest house?), without having to justify your every move.

> Living away for four years and being able to come home and have it "easy" for a while was a very appealing idea to me. It didn't hurt that my parents moved into a big new house. That definitely made it more desirable to live with them. The new house added to the overall experience, and made my time there much easier.
>
> —David, 23, Massapequa, NY

Not only that, you'll probably have the added advantage of rent-free living. But don't think you're getting off so easy. Being born to affluence comes with its own share of pitfalls. One study conducted by Martha Farnsworth Riche and featured in *American Demographics* showed that young people who come from well-to-do backgrounds often took longer to leave home because it was harder for them to re-create the lifestyle and standard of living of their parents. The rationale being: If you're used to the good life, why settle for less?

Middle-Class Dad

For those of you moving into your old bedrooms in a modest-size abode, the experience shouldn't be a terrible inconvenience. You'll probably bump into Mom and Dad on occasion, but you can still retire to the security of your room when you need to hide out. If your house is well-appointed, you can even figure out an escape route that will allow you to come and go undetected.

Poor Dad

Let us not forget the less fortunate ones, those of you who have to share a room or camp out on the family couch. For you brave souls, life at home may take a significantly weightier toll. You'll need to adapt to waking up when everyone else does and catching naps at odd hours when no one is around. If all that wasn't enough, with your family in need of extra funds, you will probably be expected to contribute monetarily for your modest digs. Of course, there is a bright side to having little to no creature comforts. The less enjoyable your experience at home, the more motivated you'll be to branch out on your own. Necessity is, after all, the mother of invention. And after a few months without privacy, you're bound to invent some excuse for getting out of there.

> I never felt like I had enough privacy because my bedroom is really painfully close to my parents' bedroom. My dad also tends to be very nosy, so it was hard to do anything on my own without everyone getting into my business. When I was in college, I was used to doing whatever I wanted when I wanted to. I had no idea living in such close quarters would be so bad.
> —Lauren, 22, Houston, TX

"1" IS THE LONELIEST NUMBER

Throughout this chapter, I've been referring to "home" as a comfy, *Leave It to Beaver*–like place with both Mom and Dad intact. But as we all know, the new American family doesn't always resemble this idyllic, TV fantasy. According to the Center for Demographic Policy, many of you grew up or lived in a single-parent household before turning 18—about 60 percent, to be exact. For those of you who have been through it, you're probably well aware of what it takes to live in a single-parent home.

On the other hand, many boomerangers are facing the prospect of coming home to one parent where there used to be two. Whether one of your parents passed away during your absence or your parents separated, you'll have to be extra-sensitive in how you deal with the new family dynamic.

When you left the family fold, your parents probably went through something called the empty nest syndrome, a time of crisis and transition where they only had each other to turn to for comfort. While some parents weathered this transition with their marriages intact or maybe even stronger for having had the experience, others didn't fare as well. According to the National Center of Health Statistics, couples who are married 30 years or longer have the highest risk of divorce. And if your experience is anything like mine, moving back in while your parents are in the process of getting a divorce or separating can be traumatic.

The most important piece of advice for you is to pare down your expectations. If your parents are recently separated or dealing with the passing of their spouse, you can hardly expect them to cater to your every whim and worry about your life crisis. They've got their own issues to contend with. It's a case of "don't ask what your parent can do for you, but what *you* can do for your parent." After all, this is probably one of the toughest times of their lives.

Another difference between living with one versus two parents is that your single parent will probably rely more heavily on you for emotional support and social interaction. Having lived with my divorced mother for several years and talked to other boomerangers in the same situation, I have come to realize that my situation was not unique. Since my mother didn't have a wide network of friends or a spouse to distract her, she would often look to my sister and me for interesting conversation and companionship. And while I enjoyed spending time with her, you may not be ready to act as your parent's sole social outlet. No matter how tight your bond is, you have to guard against your parent becoming too dependent on you. After all, you have your share of life pressures to deal with and will probably need some space to figure out where you're going.

THE BIG THREE

While the decision to park yourself at home may seem like a no-brainer or an easy out to some less-enlightened beings, millions of young adults are struggling with questions like: "Does this make me a loser?" "Am I quitter?" "Is this my life?" While all of us may be dealing with a different set of circumstances, there are some questions that are universal—three, to be exact.

Question 1. Am I a Loser?

That's easy: Of course you are. No, not really—just wanted to see if you're paying attention. In case you thought you were the only one asking this question, rest assured, you're not. Pretty much every single boomeranger I talked to struggles with doubts, insecurity, and the feeling that they are somehow less successful or together than their independently dwelling peers. They complain about not being able to hold down a job, having no significant (or even an in-significant) other, not having enough friends, and money problems.

> Moving back home was difficult. It was like swallowing my pride. It wasn't so much because I had a problem living with my father, but because it meant that I wasn't doing what I wanted to do. It was a reminder that I had lost. I definitely felt less suc-cessful than my friends. Having your own apartment and living on your own is the first sign of success. I had many friends who were working and doing what they wanted to do. I definitely had an inferiority feeling.
>
> —Harlan, 27, New York, NY

When we think of what it means to be a "success," images of a corner office, huge wads of cash, and a roomy pad where our friends and dates can gather for nights of good food and exciting conversation come to mind. Sometimes we're so focused on getting all the above that we forget all about the little things that don't come with such easy-to-read labels.

What about that time you backpacked through Chile on your

own? Or when you helped your best friend through a difficult breakup? Or what about your talent for finishing crosswords in 20 minutes or less? If you really take time to think about it, you've probably accomplished a million things in your lifetime. It's just a matter of focusing on the good stuff rather than on everything you've yet to achieve.

The key to surviving living with parents is to avoid falling into the self-pity trap. No, it's not fair that you have to move home. No, it's not fair that your generation is inheriting one of the bleakest economic legacies of the past three decades. And no, it's not fair that some of your peers have great jobs and parents to subsidize their cool apartments.

Don't forget, there's no one blueprint for success. Just because some people look as if they have it together doesn't mean that they do. If you need some time to get your bearings and figure out what you want to do, by all means—take it!

Question 2. Will I Be Stuck Here the Rest of My Life?

You don't have to be Nostradamus to predict that you won't be stuck at home your entire life. Fearing that you will never get out is akin to the thirtysomething single girl nightmare of ending up alone surrounded by cats and pints of Häagen-Dazs. The likelihood of both scenarios happening is extremely unlikely.

> When I was living at home, I wasn't really happy with the situation. But now that I'm out and can look back on it, I realize that I shouldn't have gotten so down on myself. It's important to recognize that it's not a permanent situation, and that everyone does it. Enjoy it while it lasts. I miss the beach. I miss not paying rent. I miss my brother's satellite system, where I got all these adult channels. Just because you are not on your own doesn't mean you can't *be* on your own.
>
> —Jerry, 27, Buffalo, NY

Remember, this doomsday scenario is just a projection of your fears—that you'll never find a job you love, that you'll never make any new friends, that you'll never have enough money to get your own place. It's only normal to feel this way. While it's common to worry, don't get carried away. If you don't believe me, trust in the power of statistics, which show that the majority of you will in fact be moving out eventually.

Allaying your fears is as easy as setting a goal schedule and sticking to it. By taking active steps to go after what you want, you won't have time to sit around wondering, "Is this my life?" Whether your timetable has to do with saving money or finishing grad school, creating objectives will significantly reduce your inner panic. For example, if getting into debt brought you home in the first place, figure out a savings plan in which you put away a certain amount every month. Then, calculate how long you it will take to finish saving. Is it six months? One year? Two years? So relax! You won't be home forever, just long enough to accomplish what you came home to do in the first place.

Question 3. What Will Everyone Think of Me?

> I definitely feel judged and criticized by my friends. A lot of them don't understand my feelings and they don't understand why I feel like I have to take care of my parents. Because of my age, all of my friends already have their own places so it's hard for them to understand how I can live without my own private space. But I try not to let their opinions bother me. It is my life after all.
>
> —Julie, 32, West Palm Beach, FL

Here's the thing—and it's not like I want to burst your bubble or anything—but everyone is *not* thinking about you. Your biggest nightmare may be hearing these three statements: "You live where?" "At your age?" "What's wrong with you?" But most people have more important things to sit around and ponder than why you're living at home, how long you're going to stay, and what that says about the kind of person you are.

Of course, we all have annoying friends, siblings, or acquaintances who go around spouting how terrible it is to live with your parents at our age. They claim to have done everything on their own terms, with no financial assistance of any kind, smugly arguing that today's youth are more spoiled than any group in the past. Blah, blah, blah, blah, blah!

Look deeper, however, and you'll probably find that they had a helping hand somewhere along the way. Whether it was an inside lead on a good job, a tight-knit group of friends who supported them in their hour of need, or parents who paid for their education in full, very few people can go through life claiming that they did it all on their own. And if they do, they're probably lying.

Many of you probably left jobs, relationships, and lifestyles that seemed pretty damn successful to the outside world. There are dozens of stories of people making six-figure salaries at unrewarding gigs only to move back home in an effort to find their true passion or rekindle ties with their family.

Besides, the less you worry about what people are thinking of you—whether it's that hot guy you just met at the car wash or your smug, über-successful sibling—the more energy you'll have to devote to what really matters; things like saving money, preparing a game plan for your future, and building a strong support network.

Another reason you may be so worried about being judged is because you think everyone is ahead of the game, or at least ahead of you. But how could that possibly be true if so many of you are moving back into your family homes? If all else fails, remember that there are close to 18 million other people just like you. And since you're all going through the same thing, there's really no cause for criticism.

MOVING-IN PRIMER

Despite all the odds, potential pitfalls, and warnings outlined in this chapter, most of you will have decided to make a U-turn and head back home anyway. (Why else would you be reading this book?) But before you show up on your family's doorstep, check out some strategies that will make your move back a whole lot smoother.

Step 1. Get Your Parents Involved

The last thing you want to do is spring your decision on your parents. Moving home isn't just about you! If you tell them about your situation, they may have some good advice, or you may find that they're more comfortable with giving you a loan rather than letting you move in. So if you have yet to do so, make sure to involve your parents in the decision. Besides, if you reach the decision together, you won't be as likely to blame each other when problems develop.

Step 2. Declutter Your Nest

Since you're probably moving into a space that's already furnished, you may want to consider chucking some of your furniture and belongings. That's right, it's time to embrace your inner minimalist. Unless you have a large empty basement in your parents' home, you don't want to lug a bunch of boxes into their public areas. Your poor parents will have enough trouble accommodating you, let alone all your stuff. That's not to say you should just leave your belongings on the side of the road for the garbage truck to pick up. Your best bet is to have an apartment sale or sell it off individually. Craigslist.com is a great place to sell locally. Or, try eBay.com if you think your wares can fetch a higher dollar.

Step 3. Get Organized

With all the moving and unpacking, you're liable to get a bit unorganized when it comes to your paperwork, important documents and bills. So before you move in, why not take the time to organize yourself. Put all your bills in one folder, your receipts into another, and set up yet another file for important documents like health insurance, tax information, and bank statements. That way, when you do move in, you won't waste your first week scrambling to find everything.

Step 4. Leave a Forwarding Address

In times of transition, you'll need your friends to help you through. The last thing you want to do is lose touch with the people who can make your time at home bearable. Just because some of you will be moving away from your old life doesn't mean you can't maintain your current friendships. Before you move home, make sure you collect all your friends' information: addresses, cell phone numbers, work numbers. And don't forget that it works both ways. Make sure to e-mail your new forwarding address to your entire mailing list. Even if you don't manage to keep in touch, you're bound to get a going-away party out of it.

Step 5. Thank Your Lucky Stars

The next point can't be stressed enough. Going home is *not* a right, it's a privilege. Some boomerangers (not mentioning any names here) can be incredibly self-absorbed when it comes to moving home. It's all poor me, why me? Me, me, me! Make sure not to start your life at home on this note. Instead of focusing on yourself, be grateful for the sacrifice your parents are making. No matter how great you think you are, living with you won't always be a barrel of laughs. So go ahead, invite your parents over to your apartment while you still have it for a home-cooked meal. Not only will it show how considerate you are, they'll be reminded that once upon a time you did in fact live on your own. This is one "thank you" gesture that is bound to go a long way.

The Last Supper: Top 10 Things You Should Do Before Boomeranging

Let's face it, when it comes to moving home, some of you probably have no choice in the matter. That's not to say, however, that you don't have a choice as to what you do before moving in. So without further ado, here are the top ten things you should do before moving back home:

1. Take a trip without telling anyone where you're going. Whether you're heading to Europe or driving cross-country, mum (not mom) is the word.
2. Have sex on your living-room couch. It may be a while until you can do it again in public places.
3. Throw a Moving Back Home Party for you and your friends.
4. Spend the whole day watching The Learning Channel and eating Fritos in bed. Your parents won't be as understanding as your roomie.
5. Refuse to pick up after yourself or wash the dishes for an entire week.
6. Fulfill a life fantasy, whether it's swimming with dolphins or sleeping on your roof.
7. Take photos of all your friends when you think they're not looking to create a collage for your bedroom at home.
8. If you live alone, walk around your apartment naked. It may be your last chance to let it all hang out.
9. Pay off at least one outstanding bill.
10. Toss any and all incriminating evidence—old journals, porn videos, etc.—before heading home.

3

MEET THE FAMILY, AGAIN!

I first moved home after college, when I couldn't find a job. When I finally did, my salary was only $22,000. I could barely afford the groceries. I realized I would have to stay home longer until I earned enough to move into a share in the city. A few other kids in the neighborhood moved back home for a little while, so my parents didn't think much of it. We got along, no problems. When I finally got a better-paying job in another city, I was out of there pretty quickly.

Four years later, I was working in New York—my debt was mounting, my rent increased, and my boyfriend and I had just broken up. Not only that, the company I worked for folded. I decided that I needed a break from the whole grind. When I moved back to Florida the second time, my parents were much more concerned. My mom half-joked about the "revolving door" policy. They thought I had given up and lost my motivation. That's when the arguments started. I stayed out too late, had weird friends . . . you name it! They also wanted me to go to graduate school. It took me a while to figure out what I wanted to do, and now I'm a teacher at a local high school. Our relationship is much better, but it was definitely touch and go for a while!

—Fiona, 25, Orlando, FL

Parents! Some can't live *with* you, others can't live *without* you. Conventional wisdom

had it that when you scored your college acceptance letter, that would be the last they saw of you. Yeah, right! Your parents may have anticipated, and even hoped for, the occasional pop-in, but no one expected to see their 28-year-old son back on the couch, watching *Seinfeld* reruns and hogging the remote control.

While some parents were relieved to see you go, others struggled with the empty nest syndrome. Your departure signaled a lonelier phase. Without you to kick around anymore, your once busy parents would have to rely on each other for emotional support and entertainment. The fact that their little one had grown up was cold comfort given that your getting older meant that they were maturing, too. And as we all know from being around our parents—the original Peter Pan generation—many of them struggle with the same growing pains we do.

When you finally decided to move back home, many of your parents were thrilled with the turn of events. Your arrival was a blessing. Not only could they postpone aging indefinitely, they would also have the pleasure of your lively and energetic company.

These days, being friends with our parents has become the norm. Many of us have formed new relationships with our parents that are based more on mutual interest than family obligation. We actually enjoy spending time with our folks, and actively seek them out for emotional support and guidance. Not only that, many of our parents are easy to get along with. There's the mom who can rap along to the latest Eminem release or the dad who's installed a new hot tub so that you and your friends will visit more often. No matter how independent we want to be, it's hard to resist these gestures of goodwill—especially if it means giving up a huge room, good meals, and access to the family car in favor of a dingy walk-up in a seedy part of town.

On the flip side, not all of our relationships run so smoothly. Some parents will have a harder time adjusting to your arrival. Your parting may have signaled a time when they could focus on themselves and each other. They were anxious to begin a new chapter of their lives, one that didn't involve tending to your every need. After years of raising the kids, your parents may have been looking forward to having the place to themselves. And now that you're back, that means changes for the entire household—not enough hot water, waiting to use the bathroom, and higher electricity bills. The prospect of making adjustments to their lifestyles may not be an altogether pleasant one.

While you may be kicking yourself for your bad fortune in

the parenting department, consider the fact that you may be lucky. The nagging, late-night room inspections and chore duty may be a pain now, but it will accomplish the goal of getting you out of the house faster and making you more independent. The more they nag and criticize your every move, the more motivated you'll be to save your pennies and hightail it out of there.

The truth of the matter is that your parents will be either ultra cool and sap every ounce of motivation you have to get out on your own, or extra difficult, which will make your time at home short but ultimately miserable.

It may sound grim, but there's no such thing as the perfect anything—no perfect parent, no perfect job, and no perfect relationship. If you think you have it tough, consider the fact that many of your peers don't even have their old lives to go back to. It used to be that we could leave home safely, knowing that our parents would take care of each other well into their twilight years. But now, with so many couples divorcing or separating after the kids leave, it's not unusual to return home to find only one parent where there used to be two. And with many parents simplifying their lifestyle by moving to smaller homes or even apartments in an effort to conserve resources, some are not in a position to provide their children with a safety net.

And even if your parents successfully weathered the empty nest and continued on as if you had never left, there are bound to be more changes on the horizon. The key is to be aware of the potential pitfalls of each situation.

In this chapter, we will identify the three types of parents. You'll also find coping strategies that are tailored specifically to your folks. We'll then move on to the "talking" issue, helping you to improve your communication skills in order to find mutually satisfying solutions to the most common problems. Finally, with so many of us moving home only to find our siblings grazing in the homestead, you'll also find a primer that will help you bury old grudges, cope with adult sibling rivalry, and avoid petty bickering. But first, let's find out exactly what kind of parents most of us will be dealing with.

THE COOL, THE RELUCTANT, AND THE PERMA-PARENT

Three types of parents? Can it be so simple? Can our complex, unpredictable parents really fall into three neat little categories? There may not be a user-friendly parental cheat sheet, but in the interest of saving yourself a huge headache for the next period of your life, let's create one. After all, aren't people more similar than they are different?

Many of us are laboring under the illusion that our parents are somehow abnormal. But could this really be true of all our parents? I've talked to many "adultescents," and one thing is clear: No matter how many quirks and eccentricities we ascribed to our parents, they all have the basics in common.

You should also expect some overlap in each category, with parental hybrids being the norm. And just when you thought you had it all figured out, there's the issue of your mom and dad falling

---

Who's Your Daddy? The Parent Profiler

Trying to evaluate your parents can be an exercise in futility. After all, not all parents are created equal. They have their own quirks, issues, and hang-ups—just like you.

This quiz may not be as scientific as fingerprinting or CAT scans, but it sure beats spending months trying to size up the situation. And since your mom and dad may be very different, you should take this quiz twice; once with your mom in mind and a second time for your dad. Let's get started.

1. **Your significant other's (SO) apartment is being fumigated. When you ask for permission to have him or her stay over for the night, your parents:**
A. Let your SO come over on one condition: that you let them watch movies and listen to music with the two of you.
B. Strictly forbid it, hoping it will get you out of the house faster.
C. Invite your SO to the house and spend the whole time showing off your baby pictures.

2. You've just had another argument with your boss and you need to vent. When you gripe about it to your parents, they:

A. Take you out to dinner and encourage you to join a kickboxing class to channel your anger.

B. Tell you to suck it up and get used to it. You don't want to lose this job!

C. Bake you cookies, and then offer to call your boss to straighten the whole mess out.

3. The civilized outing in the city with your friends turned into an all-night party. When you arrive home hung over and disheveled the next morning, your parents:

A. Hang on your every word, refusing to let you crash until you give them all the seedy details.

B. Hand you an AA pamphlet.

C. Tuck you in with a cold compress and two aspirins.

4. You're starving and there's nothing to eat in the house. When you complain to your parents, they:

A. Order takeout from the local Thai place. Who has time to cook?

B. Remind you that this isn't a bed-and-breakfast!

C. Ask you to make out a list of your favorite foods and promptly go grocery shopping.

5. Your sister with the cool MTV job, seven-figure fiancé, and huge loft apartment in the city comes over for dinner. Your parents:

A. Complain about not getting invites to the MTV Movie Awards.

B. Spend the whole night talking up her accomplishments, asking why you can't be more like her.

C. Talk about how dangerous it is to live in the city.

6. Your parents are planning an exotic trip to Thailand, and you've been dying to go. When you ask if you can tag along, they:

A. Are ecstatic! Now you can show them all the hip places to hang out.

B. Tell you that they need time alone to reinvigorate their marriage.

C. Check your immunization records before agreeing to let you go.

7. You've been playing your music a little too loud for the past few weeks. Your parents:

A. Ask you to burn CDs for them, too.

B. Buy you headphones for your birthday.

C. Warn you that you'll ruin your hearing.

SCORING

Mostly As: The Cool Parent

Why would you ever grow up if your parents have no intention to? That's the dilemma of being stuck with incredibly cool, fun-to-be-around parents. All your friends may be trying to crash over at your house, but you know that there's a darker side to the rosy picture. Having cool parents is not all it's cracked up to be. Sometimes a parent—not a friend—is what you need most. Still, there are many benefits, like being able to stay out late, invite friends over, and talk about major life issues without worrying about being judged. It's a lot like living with a roommate—but much cheaper.

Mostly Bs: The Reluctant Parent

Okay, so your parents may not be the warm and fuzzy types. Even if their social graces leave a lot to be desired, you may want to consider their side of the story. The idea of having one of their brood back in the fold makes them apprehensive. They probably had plans of their own— taking cooking classes, redecorating the house—plans that your arrival has postponed. So before you start complaining about your draw in the genetic lottery, take a moment to consider the matter from their perspective.

Mostly Cs: The Perma-Parent

These parents live to baby and nurture you. These are the same people who cried when you went to college, sent you one care package after another, and worried about you every waking moment. While it's nice to feel cared for, it's all too easy to slip into a state of inertia. Now that you're back, perma-parents have no intention of treating you like an adult. Expect home-cooked meals and chore-free living. These folks will go out of their way to make you feel all warm and cozy, hoping that you never leave. And that's the danger—you might never want to.

into separate groups—while some of you may find that both parents fit cozily into one profile, others will see that when it comes to parenting styles, opposites really do attract.

And finally, if you're living in a single-parent home, the same parenting categories apply. Their manifestations, however, may be that much more pronounced, since your parent doesn't have a spouse to balance him or her out.

Consider it time well spent to read all three parental descriptions. And remember to use the guidelines loosely. Parents cannot be neatly boxed up and put away on a shelf, no matter how much we sometimes want to do exactly that.

THE COOL PARENT

Boomerang parents have come a long way. They're color coordinated, up on all the latest celebrity gossip, and know the difference between a trucker cap and a baseball hat. All that training finally paid off. Congratulations! These specimens of parenthood are definitely not like your grandparents' generation, who as a result of the Depression and World War II were known to adopt a stricter, more disciplinarian approach to parenting. Times were tough back then, and you could bet your parents were taught that in order to succeed, they would have to work overtime.

Having grown up in the era of love, peace, and the occasional demonstration, your parents are probably much cooler than you think. In fact, most "cool" parents want nothing more than to see their offspring happy and satisfied. Raising well-rounded, evolved kids has been their main priority. Many of them figure that all their hard work is well worth the effort if their kids have the chance to find their true calling and passion. And if that means having us move back home, then so be it. Our cool, hipster parent would do anything to see us happy. Their mantra? "Be happy, dammit!"

Still, no matter how comforting, there's a price to pay for unconditional acceptance. During our teenage years, many cool parents had trouble setting limits, overindulging our every whim. They let us watch music videos, when we should have been doing homework. They gave us a feeling of entitlement, when they should have been preparing us for a much bleaker economic picture. But even if their ways were too lax at times, the result is that they have made their homes that much more welcoming and inviting. Instead of having to call and badger us for lunch dates, *we're* the ones who are always seeking them out, hungry for that elusive experience of unconditional friendship and security.

Simply put, the age gap is just not as big a factor as it used to be. Many of our so-called "cool" parents listen to the same music we do, shop at the same stores, and even talk like us. And while it may produce its share of humorous moments, you've got to love the fact that they're trying so hard. In a world where friends come and go and life can sometimes move too fast to establish solid, life-long bonds, having a relationship, however chummy, with our parents is definitely something to be proud of.

Take Lila, for example. Having lived with her mother for over six years as a roommate, she never considered moving out until her thirtieth birthday.

> Living with my mother wasn't at all like living at home. My parents got divorced right after I graduated college, and moving in with her just seemed like the thing to do. We even bought a place together, where each of us paid a share of the monthly costs. It was like having a roommate, but better. It wasn't like she would ever tell me what to do, who to go out with, what to wear. She pretty much did the same things I did—staying up late to watch movies, eating ice cream for dinner (everything I loved to do). When I finally moved into a new place with a roommate, I found myself coming back to my mom's at least four times a week to watch reality shows and eat takeout together. Even after living on my own for a while, I probably spend more time at her place than I do at mine. But that's okay, because we're really close. Our relationship doesn't have to change just because I moved out.
>
> —Lila, 32, Durfield, IL

Parent Prescription 1. Draw a Line in the Sand

If you find that your parents are incapable or simply unwilling to set boundaries, you'll have to do the dirty work for them. They aren't used to acting like conventional parents and would much rather be your friends. It's important that you be gentle and work on them slowly. If your parents want to hang out with you and your friends, and you'd like some time on your own, say so. Even if you don't mind worlds colliding and would like nothing better than to include your 'rents, resist the impulse to do that. It's very important that you have your social network and that they have theirs. Don't forget to throw in the kind gesture or two. Arrange another time when you and your parents can be together one-on-one over brunch or dinner. They'll appreciate the sentiment, and you'll have established a much-needed boundary in an otherwise blurry family dynamic.

Parent Prescription 2. Don't Believe the Hype

All cool parents think that their kid is the most creative, insightful, and hip individual they've ever met. Problem is, the cooler your parents think you are, the more time they'll want to spend with you. And that means less privacy for you. As much as you'd like to believe your own cool rep—don't! You have to realize that besides your other equally cutting-edge siblings, you're their one link to the outside world of young, crazy kids. Of course they're going to think that you're so au courant. Remember when you entered your senior year in high school? You were cool just by virtue of being older. And now that you're moving back home, you're cool just by virtue of being younger. Still, it's probably hard for you to give up the limelight. Our egos get used to our parents' constant attention. But the sooner you stop believing your parents' hype, the sooner you can stop deluding yourself. Go on, do it. Tell your parents you're not as cool as they think you are. They may not believe you, but it's worth a shot.

Parent Prescription 3. Parents Are People, Too!

While it may feel great to have your parents fawn all over you in their attempts to embrace their own coolness, your job is to encourage them to find out who *they* really are. Most cool parents want to live vicariously through you in a futile effort to avoid growing up. It's your job to show them that they have a lot going for them, as well. Make an effort to focus on them. Ask about their hobbies, forgotten dreams, even past loves (if you can stomach it). They may be uncomfortable at first, preferring to talk about you, but they'll get the hang of it eventually. The more you encourage them to open up, the more likely that they'll rediscover themselves and develop new interests and hobbies. Only then can they stop trying to emulate their children and embrace the mature, dynamic individuals hiding inside.

> I'm living at home now, but this isn't the first stint I've done. I moved back home a total of four times since college. The first time right after graduating. The second time after leaving a going-nowhere job in New York. The third time after having to work as a movie extra to pay the bills. And the fourth time, after turning down a promotion at an entertainment magazine. All in all, my parents have been really great. They're celebrating their "inner child" through me. We've had some great parties, with their friends and my friends singing along to Led Zeppelin. But we've always been really close and open, so it's not so different. At this point, I couldn't imagine living anywhere else.
> —Sophie, 27, Cambridge, MA

You Know You're Too Close to Your Parents When . . .

It's getting more and more accepted to be friends with our parents. Of course, there is such a thing as being *too* close. Cross that line and you're bordering on creepy. If you're doing any of the following, you may need either to exorcise your parents or exercise your independence.

- ⇁ You always ask your parents before making plans with your friends.
- ⇁ You're double-dating with Mom or Dad.
- ⇁ Your last three vacations were road trips with Mom, Dad, and little sis/bro.
- ⇁ You call your parents to consult on every decision, from what nail polish to buy to what to order at a restaurant.
- ⇁ You'd rather spend the night playing board games with the family than hang out with your boyfriend/girlfriend.
- ⇁ You're still knocking on their door every time there's a thunderstorm.
- ⇁ Instead of going out to lunch with your coworkers, you drive home a half hour each way to eat lunch with your parents.

THE RELUCTANT PARENT

After years of changing your dirty diapers, carting you to and from soccer practice, and barely surviving your sullen teenage phase, many parents are dying for a break. They look forward to their golden years when the house is finally quiet, the fridge is well stocked, and they can sleep soundly knowing they won't be interrupted in the middle of the night by your clamorous arrival. Who knows, they may even want to spend some quality time with each other. Anyone who's been there knows: Raising kids is no easy feat. So when the day comes that you're finally on your own, safely tucked away in your apartment, working full-time and supporting yourself, many parents quietly rejoice at their good fortune. Can you blame them?

Most of our parents were married, working toward a pension, and putting away their pennies for our college funds long before they were 25. By the time you learned to balance your checkbook, they were already navigating the new roles of adulthood. The option of moving back home with their folks was simply not available or too strange to consider.

Today's climate is much different. Economically, we're in no position to accomplish the same feats as our parents, and emotionally, many of us aren't ready to commit to raising a family. Millions of us have been forced into a state of delayed adulthood. While *we* are no strangers to this new reality, some parents are living in a bit of a time warp. After all, unlike us, they're not trying to make it for the first time, and probably have a vastly different idea of what it means to be successful and mature.

Despite more and more adultolescents returning to the family fold, some parents still think this is the exception rather than the rule. When they sent you off to college, they weren't prepared to see you home so soon. Many of them converted your bedrooms into offices, dens, or home gyms. You can imagine their surprise to see you on their doorstep with all your worldly possessions in tow.

My parents were definitely surprised, but I explained to them that it wasn't my choice, that if I had a job straight out of school and could afford to move out immediately, I probably would have. The respect issue came up since I was used to having the freedom I experienced in college. So, we butted heads a bit. I refused to revert to my high school relationship with them and made them adjust to a new relationship—one that was on more equal footing. The staying-out-late issue became a problem, and they gave me that whole "don't use the house as a hotel" speech, but I made compromises by curbing my partying and not introducing them to girls I dated.

—Ben, 24, Port Washington, NY

Parent Prescription 1. Burst Their Bubble

Most parents don't realize just how tough it is to make it in this day and age. Think about it. Could they really afford their house or apartment with real estate prices being what they are today? Could they really bounce back as quickly as you did after being laid off three times in the past five years? Certainly they had their own share of hardships to deal with, but so do you. Your parents need to be made aware of how different the world has become.

Instead of blaming your parents for their ignorance, why not take some time to educate them? Print out some articles about the rising cost of housing, compile some stats on unemployment, and read to them from the first chapter of this book. They probably have no idea how many young adults are on their way back home. Once they get the facts, they may be much more likely to cut you some slack.

Parent Prescription 2. Don't Back Down

While diplomacy always reigns supreme, a firm position can sometimes show bossy parents that you mean business, too. Some parents still feel entitled to play the "my house, my rules" card. Now that you're all grown up, you have to let them know that you're no longer a kid, and that you're willing to compromise—to a point. For every rule they set, make an equally firm counterpoint. If there's absolutely no way you're going to be able to clean your room every day, tell them so up front. Explain that you'll make every effort to keep the public areas tidy, but you are old enough to manage your personal clutter. If their chore schedule seems more like indentured servitude, create an alternate plan that shows you're in control. A little tough love can work wonders with some parents. Funny thing is, they're probably saying the same thing about you.

Parent Prescription 3. Make Them Proud

Your parents aren't ogres. It just may be that they're in dire need of an ego boost of their own. Think about it: Many reluctant parents see your return home as a failing on their part. Their very success as a parent is being threatened. They hear stories about so-and-so's son doing so well, and worry that their parenting skills somehow contributed to your predicament. It's your job to help them see otherwise.

Instead of sleeping in late every day, why not get up early and make your mom lunch before she heads off to work? Instead of being asked to do the dishes and other chores, why not have them done before your parents come home? And don't wait until asked to talk about your progress. Make a point of discussing your job search, extra income ideas, and other life-improvement plans as often as possible. Once they see that you're making an effort, they'll realize that they succeeded as parents, after all.

THE PERMA-PARENT

There's no explaining it: While some parents can't wait to get us out of the house, others balk at the prospect of their little ones growing up. In fact, many of these perma-parents are in permanent denial, refusing to acknowledge our new adult status. No matter how many jobs we've held, businesses we've run, relationships we've been in and out of, they still want to hold our hand when we cross the street.

As parents, it's easy to get caught up in the role of protector and nurturer. That's what they're supposed to do, after all. They've spent so much time worrying about feeding us, supporting us, and helping us that they eventually forget how to relate to us as independent people.

> They were happy that I was there. They like having me close to them, especially because I'm the baby of the family. I guess it gets harder for parents when all their children move out of the house—all of a sudden it's like what happened to my life. Having me around, they didn't have to freak out about their life changing so dramatically.
>
> —David, 26, Buffalo, NY

The perma-parent has the hardest time dealing with the empty nest syndrome. Instead of being thrilled by your courageous flight into the great unknown, they missed having someone to care for. Many parents experience an extreme feeling of loss and have no idea what to do with themselves. Is it any wonder that they welcome us so readily when we return home?

The idea of having us back in the fold gives them a whole new lease on life. They finally get to do what they do best: parent us. They mill around, asking us if we want more snacks, more privacy, more Flintstones chewable vitamins. Problem is, you're no longer a child. You've probably been on your own for a while and have gotten used to tying your own shoes and doing your own cooking and laundry.

Perma-parents have a way of making us feel as if we're right back where we started. And while that can feel good at times, especially after the world has dealt us a blow, it can also be debilitating to our sense of self-sufficiency. We begin to crave the comfort and security, forgetting that we are in fact fully functioning adults. It's all too easy to regress when your mom reminds you to eat your veggies and brings you hot milk before bed. But reverting back to childhood is the last thing we want to do, especially when we're desperately trying to get our lives back on track.

> I've always had a close relationship with my mom. But when I moved in with her, she was really trying to mother me. She would always tell me to wear something warm (in 80 degree weather) or eat before I left. The woman fed me like crazy. I had to admit that after a while, I did regress a little. I got lazier and

pushed off doing things I would normally do for myself, like cooking dinner or grocery shopping. Living on my own for so long, I wasn't used to being mothered. It was a little bit annoying, but it did feel good for a while.

—Cory, 25, Skokie, IL

Parent Prescription 1. Do It Yourself

It's unavoidable; you move back home full of plans to maintain your schedule and complete all your to-dos, only to find that your parents are more than glad to do your laundry, cook your dinners, and even scour the classifieds in search of your new job. How in the world are you ever going to get back on your feet if your parents are doing all the heavy lifting for you? Your first step is to talk the matter through. Thank them for being so helpful, but explain that you're ready to be responsible for yourself. Then walk the walk. Take care of all your own responsibilities so your parents don't beat you to the punch. That means cleaning up after yourself, ironing your own shirts, and restocking the fridge. No matter how much they like babying you, your actions should tell them that you're ready to be treated as an adult.

Parent Prescription 2. Turn the Tables

In the spirit of *Freaky Friday*, why not turn the tables on your parents by treating them like little kids? Make them breakfast in bed, do their laundry, and insist that they brush their teeth before going to bed. They may protest at first, but everyone loves to be pampered. Even if they don't take to your new strategy, at least they'll understand what it feels like to be treated like an infant. So go ahead and spoil them like the big babies they are. Believe me, they'll never have it so good again.

Parent Prescription 3. Redirect Their Energy

If you want to avoid becoming your family's pet project, you'll need to find them a new one. Since your perma-parents may be going through a midlife slump, use your time at home to come up with new ways to occupy them. Show them there's more to life than being a parent. Sign them up for classes, teach them how to make new friends online, take them out to museums—you may even consider adopting a new family pet. Redirecting their energy to other activities can be just the thing to get some breathing space of your own.

CAN WE TALK?

Now that you have a better idea of what makes your parents tick, you can start on improving other areas of your relationship. One of the main factors leading to a satisfying home life is how well you communicate. Learning to negotiate, staying calm in the face of conflict, and using discretion are key tools that will prevent built-up resentment. Whether you're an ace communicator or are still resorting to pouting to get your way, all of us could use a refresher course from time to time. After all, while lines like "You're not the boss of me!" "Leave me alone!" and "I hate you!" may have gotten your point across in the past, your new adult status requires that you find a more appropriate way to express yourself.

> I never had issues talking to my mom, but my dad was a different story. We butted heads all through high school, and my strategy for moving back home was to avoid him altogether. Seeing my mom and me chat away, I think he began feeling bad about [us] not having a relationship. He started asking me questions about my life. At first I was put off and didn't want to talk. But my mom encouraged me to give him a chance. Eventually we were talking about all kinds of things: politics, personal finances, and then moved on to more personal topics like my life direction and career goals. He even helped me file my taxes so I ended up saving more money. I'm kind of glad I moved back. If I hadn't, I'd never have been forced to get to know my dad.
>
> —Brett, 26, San Diego, CA

Form a Habit

Don't wait until there's a problem to start talking. Communicating with your folks should come as naturally as breathing, eating, and sleeping. And now that you're all under one roof, it's a good idea to have these little chats more often. Of course, not all families are used to having regular sit-downs. Don't feel weird if you and your parents get a bit tongue-tied at first. It's only natural to feel awkward. One great tip to get the ball rolling is to start on neutral ground. Bring up an article or a book that relates to an issue you're dealing with, something like, "I was just reading about so and so . . ." Your parents are bound to chime in on the subject, and you won't have to deal with the discomfort of long silences over the dinner table.

Volunteer Information

Don't make your parents feel as if they're prying. The best way to put the relationship on an equal footing is to treat them sort of like friends. If you act as secretive as when you were in high school, everyone will revert to familiar but outworn roles. Whether it was your first heartbreak or being ostracized by your so-called friends, we all had those times when we refused to talk to our parents. Well, things have changed. Hopefully, you've been honest with your folks about what brought you back to their doorstep. It may have been humbling, but you had no choice except to give them the whole story. It will be very important to keep your parents informed about what's happening in your life during your stay. Instead of making them bang down your door, make an effort to come out and talk once in a while.

Learn the Art of Negotiation

Having lived on your own, it's easy to feel a sense of entitlement. We're used to coming and going as we please, so it's not uncommon that we become defensive and feel as if we have to guard our turf. The last thing you want to do is to make demands, expecting that your parents will go out of their way to please you. After all, they'll be giving up a lot, too. Their concerns are just as valid as yours. The key is to negotiate in a way that makes both parties feel that their needs are being met. Take time to listen to them to make sure that all sides are given equal weight. The best way to do that is to create a priorities list. If your main priority is to have access to the family car, place that at the top of your list. If your parents place a high value on rent contribution, make sure they specify that. As you go down the list, look for artful compromises. For instance, pay a little extra rent for the privilege of using the car more often. That way, both you and your parents can walk away from the bargaining table feeling like winners.

> When I moved back home, my main concern was space. I would have to live with both my grandparents, my younger brother, and my parents. I got used to having my own room, even if it did mean having to live with two roommates. I knew that I needed my privacy, so I offered to convert the basement into a living area for myself. At the time, it was jam-packed with my parents' junk, things that they never used. But when I offered to clean it out and weatherproof it myself, they were really against it. My mom suddenly became very defensive about getting rid of all her things, and we ended up fighting about it for a month. That's when I had an idea of putting the stuff up for sale on eBay. I showed my parents the site, and they agreed if I could make $1,000 off it, they would let me sell the stuff. It took a while, but I eventually sold it all, with a profit of $1,600. They were happy with the extra cash, and I got a private place to stay.
> —Karen, 25, Fort Lee, NJ

Be a Zen Master

There are bound to be things about your parents that push your buttons, and vice versa. It's important that you don't lose your cool. If you ask to be treated like an adult, be prepared to act like one. Channeling your inner Buddha means not throwing a fit just because something doesn't go your way. Even if you feel that your parents are being too strict or unreasonable, you can still maintain a calm demeanor. It's unrealistic to expect that everything will go smoothly. There are bound to be a few rough edges to polish off. If the situation feels tense and on the brink of an emotional explosion, make an effort to steer the conversation back to the basics. What are the basics, you ask? The fact that for better or worse, you're all in this together. If the new living arrangement is going to work, both sides will need to maintain a calm and respectful attitude toward each other.

Keep It in the Family

Dishing to your friends about your boss, dates, and relatives may have helped you deal in the past, but now that you're back home, reconsider spilling all your family secrets. Even if you don't feel es-

---

The Parent Problem Solver

All parents, no matter how well meaning, will make mistakes from time to time. Refer to this problem solver for quick solutions to the most common parental offenses.

Problem: *Nagging* Clean up your room! Pay your bills! Get a job! The constant nagging is driving you crazy.
Solution: Ask them to make a list of all their complaints. Then get together to create a schedule for when you'll accomplish everything. Contrary to popular belief, your parents don't enjoy nagging you. They just want to know things are getting done.

Problem: *Making Comparisons* Some parents are always reminding you of a cousin who's a big-time lawyer or that next-door neighbor's kid who just happened to have cured cancer.
Solution: Level with them. Explain that Rome wasn't built in one day and that everyone has his or her own timeline for success. Make sure they know how bad you feel when they compare you to others. They may not even be aware of what they're doing.

Problem: *Guilt Trips* "What will become of me if you leave?" "If you love me, you'd . . . " Some parents lay guilt trips like chickens lay eggs.
Solution: Don't respond. If you try to console them, they'll feel gratified by the attention, which is what they really want in the first place. Instead, help them feel more confident by complimenting their independence and ability to manage the household on their own.

Problem: *Doomsday Tactics* Their warnings about the dangers of walking home alone, living on your own, or even flying the friendly skies are beginning to make you paranoid.
Solution: Remind them that most accidents occur around the home. If that doesn't work, make it clear that you're aware of the safety concerns, but that you're not about to stop living your life for fear of "what if?"

pecially loyal toward your clan, talking behind their backs with your friends can create a me-against-them mentality. It's a bad habit that can escalate an already tense situation. The best way to deal with family is through direct, heart-to-heart talks. Like it or not, you should try to see your parents as new allies who deserve your loyalty. After all, they did take you in during your hour of need. That has to be worth something, right?

> For the most part, we get along great. When I moved home after my car accident, my mom and dad went out of their way to get me back on my feet. Problem was they became really overprotective. I know they were still shocked about the accident, but life goes on. My mom watched the news constantly, and would report to me about other accidents and natural disasters. Even though I was ready to move out after a year, my parents insisted that I stay a few more months to get stronger. It was tough convincing them that I was ready to go, but I knew that a few more weeks of my mom reading to me from the newspaper, and I'd probably have lost my mind.
>
> —Mara, 24, Chicago, IL

OH BROTHER! THE SIBLING DILEMMA

I knew my brother would be a huge pain in the neck when I moved home. He's 28 years old, never lived on his own, and spends all his money on partying instead of helping with rent. We've never been really close. I had really strong feelings about the fact that he's not doing enough in his life and wasting all his talents. Just as I suspected, we fought the first few months when I moved in. It was horrible. He was so lazy and took advantage of our mom. I felt like it was either me or him—one of us would have to move out. Our parents were also getting worn down with all our fighting. They couldn't stand seeing their kids go at it. I decided that I would have to move out, and when I told my brother about it, he got really sad. I guess he kind of liked having me around, though he never showed it. He promised that if I stayed he would help out around the house more and try to be nicer to our parents. And while things were far from perfect, we did get along better after that.

—Dan, 26, Staten Island, NY

With all this talk of getting along with parents, let's not forget about our dear brothers and sisters. Remember *The Royal Tenenbaums?* One genius prodigy moves back into the family mansion, only to be followed by all the others. Your sibling probably wants a piece of the action, too. "If she/he gets to move in, why can't I?" will be their battle cry. And rightfully so. What, did you think *you* would be the only one to benefit from all those household perks? So unless you're an only child, remember, where there's one boomeranger, there's bound to be two, or three, or four. That's right, prepare to make some room!

As any of us lucky enough to be born with brothers and sisters know, getting along and going along isn't always easy. Whether you're in junior high, high school, college, or long moved on to the real world, there's always that push and pull that characterizes even the healthiest sibling relationships. Having lived with my sister, older by one year, for the entire duration of my twenties, I can attest to some of the hardships you will be facing. Not only did we live together, we worked together. Can you imagine the possibilities? Here's how our day went down:

10:00 A.M.	Finish breakfast
10:30 A.M.	Argue about who cleans up
11:30 A.M.	Make up quickly due to overriding urge to go shopping
3:00 P.M.	Argue over who stepped on whose foot while walking
8:00 P.M.	Reconcile over several glasses of sangria at downtown bar
1:00 A.M.	Fall asleep angry due to one final big fight over who did more work that day

I can only shake my head in wonder as to how my poor mother put up with all of it (though I secretly think it brought some much-needed drama into her life).

Very few boomerangers prepare themselves to deal with the sibs when they return home. You've probably been more worried about dealing with your parents, getting out of debt, or figuring out how you ended up back home in the first place. It won't help matters any if you have a sibling at home whom you don't get along with. Of course, with every downside, there's bound to be some benefits. While some of you can't spend one hour in the same room together, others will find that living with adult siblings can be a major boon. Not only will you have a ready-made friend with whom you can go out, you'll also have someone to support you when the going gets tough.

Living with your siblings as an adult may also help you get over those old childhood traumas. Whether one is an older, middle, or younger child, we're all carrying some grudge against our siblings. The older kid feels neglected, the middle feels invisible, and the younger is usually the one everyone else picked on. You see, we're all in this together. So isn't it time to lay some of those grudges to rest? After all, when your parents are long gone, it will be you and your siblings until the end—provided, of course, you don't kill each other first.

TOP FIVE SIBLING COMPLAINTS

Ever since Cain slew Abel and Romulus killed Remus, siblings have gotten a bad rap for creating havoc. Whether toppling empires or fighting for bathroom space, there's always some rift, rancor, or unresolved grudge that needs to be addressed. While some sibling discord dissolves over time, other feuds can continue and even exacerbate with the years.

Whether your siblings took out all their teenage angst on you or you constantly upstaged them with your "cute-as-a-button" routine, you're probably both responsible for making each other's life a wee bit miserable. So now that all of you are back home again, isn't it time to let bygones be bygones? Here are some ways to do just that.

1. **Sibling Rivalry.** So what if your older brother has a kick-ass job at *Rolling Stone*? Who cares if your younger sister rocked her MCATs? Just because they're doing well doesn't mean *you* aren't. You know rivalry is a problem when the happiness of your sib leads to nothing but misery for you. But don't forget, there are plenty of kudos to go around. In fact, a little healthy competition can be just the motivation

you need to get you off the couch and earn some accolades of your own. Of course, if your sibling is intent on rubbing your nose in his or her accomplishments, you're entitled to feel some resentment. But you needn't take the bait. Instead of engaging in the one-upmanship, do your best to ignore your sib's comments. An even better strategy would be to take your gloating sib out for a celebratory dinner. Not only will it catch the little bragger off guard, celebrating each other's accomplishments also may become a new family tradition.

2. **What's the Difference?** She's the funny one. He's the cute one. She's the hardworking one. He's the outgoing one. Too many of us compensate and take on different traits in an effort to seem as if we're nothing like our sibs. Growing up, all of us wanted to be special, and this was our way of proclaiming our uniqueness to the world. But since you've been gone, you may have redefined yourself as all of the above—as the smart one, the funny one, the cute one, *and* the outgoing one. Good for you! But now that you're home and faced with your sibling, you may be prone to reverting back to old roles that no longer fit who you are. So how do you deal with it? Embrace all these qualities within yourself and make sure you do the same with your sibling. Take turns being smart, funny, and interesting. With all the focus on celebrating the differences, why not focus on the similarities? You can argue about who has better taste in movies, but in the end both of you are cinema buffs. You can bicker about who forgot to clean up the kitchen, but in the end both of you hate cleaning the kitchen. Look for the common ground—all of us are more similar than we are different. And that's especially true of you and your siblings. After all, you *do* share the same gene pool. That should count for something, right?

3. **Mom Always Loved You Best!** Even if your parents did a bang-up job trying to make all of you feel equally loved, there's always one person in the family who feels like the "have not." After all, parents aren't perfect, and as much as they try, they don't always succeed in treating their kids the same. Some of you may feel like your siblings can do no wrong in your parents' eyes, while you're always in the dog house. No matter who feels as if they're not getting their fair share of

ELINA FURMAN

love, respect, or appreciation, you'll all need to deal with these issues so that they do not threaten your current relationship. If you do feel that there is some inequality, make a point to talk about it with your parents—*not* your sib. After all, despite the resentment you feel for him/her/them, your parents are the real culprits here. Make sure to tell them that their behavior is causing some problems, and be specific about some of the instances in which you feel you were treated unfairly. And while it won't right the skewed family dynamic overnight, their behavior may improve once they're aware of what's bothering you.

4. **Anger Management.** For some reason, siblings know how to push our buttons like no other. They know how to say just the perfect thing to make you go from calm and happy to fuming angry in three seconds flat. With so much history between you, it's not surprising that they know all your weak points and vulnerabilities. It's like having your dirty laundry aired time and time again, regardless of how many times you tell them to stop. But fighting with your sibling won't make your time at home any more pleasant. Besides, think about your poor parents. They've already endured all those years of bickering. Do you really want to put them through all that again? Assuming your answer is no, you'll need to craft a strategy for every time your sibling reminds you of when you crashed the car or that fateful day you were suspended from school. When it comes to your siblings dredging up your unsavory past, you need to be clear about what you will and won't tolerate. While you may be tempted to retort with some equally salacious bits of gossip or even threaten them verbally, you'll only be hurting yourself in the end. The best way to deal with this childish behavior is to walk away. Just tell the troublemaker that you won't stand for such below-the-belt remarks and get out of there before you lose your cool.

5. **The Cinderella Syndrome.** One of the most prevalent complaints is when one sibling fails to pull his/her weight in the household. It can be very frustrating when you're doing all the chores, paying rent, and spending time with your parents and your sibling is just loafing around the house watching the paint dry. If that's the case in your

house, try to get your parents involved. Encourage them to establish guidelines and rules about household chores and financial contributions. But make sure you tell your parents to keep you out of the discussion. The last thing you want is to make your sibling feel as if everyone is ganging up against him/her.

A FINAL NOTE

Whether your parents are still threatening eviction if you don't get your act together or your siblings are driving you crazy, you've hopefully come away with a better understanding of who they are as people. No matter how you've interacted in the past, good communication skills, dependable actions, and mutual respect can go a long way toward making your relationships more satisfying. Your newfound skills may even change the family dynamic, allowing each party to see each other in a new way.

In the course of a lifetime, our relationship with our families will continue to evolve, forcing us to relate to one another on different terms each time. Your parents will get older, retire, and may even need your assistance someday. Your formerly pesky siblings may mature, wise up, and even become a source of immense emotional support for you.

It's important to remember that change is constant; the things we take for granted today may not be around tomorrow. The more we learn to relate to each other as equals, the better our chance of forming an enduring bond that will support us through the ups and downs that are an inevitable part of life.

Even if you're cursing your fate of having to move back home, consider how lucky you are to be able to get to know your parents and siblings as an adult. Cohabitating with parents may not be as glamorous as living a freewheeling lifestyle, but don't be surprised if one day you're actually grateful for having had the opportunity.

4

THERE'S NO PLACE LIKE HOME ... OR IS THERE?

At first my parents tried to control certain actions of mine solely because I was financially dependent on them. In the beginning, I didn't help with chores as much as I should have and I didn't spend a lot of time with them. So when they told me about how they felt, I listened carefully and we fixed the situation. After that our relationship definitely improved. I had to relearn how to live under their rules and to help out around the house. Thanks to their understanding and patience with me, it was an easy transition for me. We became close again and have a great level of mutual respect for each other. They are more relaxed and trust me more. I am allowed to do what I want, and they trust me to make good decisions. The space they gave me and their desire to be a bigger part of my life made the transition considerably easier.

—Ryan, 23, New York, NY

No matter how you slice it, dice it, or mash it, you and your folks are going to have to set some ground rules pronto. If you hope to have any chance of co-existing in peace and loving harmony, then don't wait another minute to lay down the law. No matter what authority issues you're still harboring from your past or how much you hate the idea of following rules, you'll have to accept a higher power than yourself. It may not be easy to admit it, but you're on your parents' turf now and making some concessions will be unavoidable.

Having said that, living at home the second time around doesn't mean having to sacrifice all the freedoms and privileges that come with a separate dwelling. Not only that, parents shouldn't have to give up their lifestyles or go broke to support your grazing habits.

While some parents may be ultra strict about enforcing rules, there are ways to cohabit so both parties are happy with the arrangement. As trite as it may sound, it's all about creating a win-win scenario, in which both you and your parents feel good about living together. The key to having a harmonious family life and a smoothly running household is to discuss issues before they become problems. Not only will you be able to find that your everyday life is running more smoothly, you may even grow to respect your parents more—and vice versa.

Besides this added bonus, figuring out how you can contribute to the household will give you a sense of accomplishment. It can help you feel more mature at a time when many of you feel as if you're taking a backward step in your lives. You'll feel instantly older, more self-determined, and helpful. You may even find that other parts of your life, including career and personal matters, function better when you take on extra responsibilities on the home front.

> Even though I've lived with my mom for many years, I actually think I'm more self-sufficient than many of my friends who are on their own. For instance, I do my own grocery shopping, my own laundry, walk our dog three times day, contribute toward household expenses, and figure out all the "man of the house" stuff like the cable box, the fuse box, and moving heavy stuff. I feel really good about myself since many of my single and divorced friends still need everything done for them.
>
> —Kirsten, 35, Boston, MA

Of course you can't expect to iron out all the details overnight. Finding a balance at home will require patience, tolerance, and a willingness to compromise on both sides. But with a little planning, and a lot of communication, boomerangers and their parents can find that living together can save money, cut down on chores, and even bring everyone closer together.

LAYING DOWN THE LAW

Very few families can subsist on good communication and understanding alone. When it comes down to it, it's much better for boomerangers to know what's expected of them at the outset in order to stop angry and resentful feelings from building up. No matter how much you hate setting, following, or enforcing rules, you'll have to acclimate yourself to the idea that you'll be expected to help out from time to time.

> When I moved home, I figured things would work like they used to. My mom pretty much did everything around the house [while I was] growing up, and my dad would fix stuff that needed maintenance. Except for cleaning my room once a month or so, I really wasn't responsible for much. That's why I was surprised that my mom was so mad about me not helping out. I guess she had gotten used to only cleaning up after herself and my dad. After a couple of weeks at home, they pretty much laid it on the line and said that if I didn't help out, I'd have to find a new place to live.
>
> —Mike, 29, Astoria, NY

With so many boomerangers being in the dark about how strict their parents are going to be, you should start hashing out the family rules well in advance of your move-in date. If you wait to negotiate the terms of your agreement, you'll be putting yourself in a vulnerable position. Your parents know you won't want to move out so soon after arriving, and will probably try to play hardball.

Still, if you're already in the house and realize that you can't thrive under their regime, all is not lost. You can still bargain your way into getting some household perks. But don't wait till both you and your parents are ready to wage war. Talking about problems when all of you are tired, angry, and resentful is never a good idea.

To make the whole process smoother, read on to find out about the most frequently debated points among boomerangers and parents. Once you iron out these issues, you'll find life at home to be that much smoother.

Cleanup Duty

Only you know if you're really a slob or just casually messy. But whatever your cleanliness quotient is, one thing is certain—your parents shouldn't have to trail after you with a broom and dustpan. Hopefully, having lived on your own for a while, you've become somewhat responsible about keeping things tidy. And now that you're home, there's absolutely no reason to stop. Just because Mom or Dad used to do all the heavy lifting doesn't mean you should revert back to the old ways. You don't want to start replacing good habits with bad ones, especially since you'll be on your own again soon enough and will need to remember how to clean up after yourself.

When it comes to your bedroom, some of you may be laboring under the false notion that since it's your room, you have the power to decide how messy it gets. It's the old "state versus federal law" business. But no matter where your room is located, you're still under your parents' jurisdiction, which means that they ultimately have the final say about what happens there.

Besides cleaning your room and any public areas of the house in which you make a mess, which should be your topmost priority, your parents will probably want you to clean up after your meals, do the dishes, vacuum, and take out the garbage. One good tip for keeping the house clean is to assign each family member chores on different days of the week. For instance, you would be responsible for all the cleanup chores on Mondays, Wednesdays, and Fridays, your dad on Tuesdays and Sundays, and your mom on Thursdays and Saturday. It's a lot easier than trying to keep track of who did what. Of course this system won't work for everyone, so come up with one that works for you and your family.

Points to ponder:

- Which chores will you be responsible for?
- Who will do the housework on which days of the week?
- What consequences, if any, will be enforced if the chores aren't completed?

Laundry

While your parents may have had no other choice but to wash your tighty-whities when you were a tyke, those days are long gone. Leaving this ungrateful chore to your parents won't make you feel like a grown-up. And besides, if your mom is always finding your dirty laundry mixed in with hers she may grow tired of your antics and start picking on you for other trivial reasons. And don't even think about offering to pay your parents a dollar per pound to do your laundry. Despite the fact that many of us big-city boomerangers have gotten spoiled by drop-off laundry services, your parents won't appreciate your offer, however generous. In the end, your best bet is to thank your lucky stars that you have a free washer/dryer at your disposal and just do it yourself. Or even better, why not pitch in and do the family's laundry once in a while. This is one chore they won't miss.

Points to ponder:

> Who will be responsible for buying laundry detergent?
> How many times a month will you be doing laundry?
> On what days of the week and at what time will you do your laundry?
> How will you keep your laundry separate from the rest of the family's?

The Self-Stocking Refrigerator

As kids, many of us assumed that the fridge restocked itself. We would hang out for hours exploring its contents, and wonder why there was always a shortage of OJ. As adults, we realize that the Jetsons fantasy we were weaned on just doesn't exist. In order to fill the fridge, one must actually leave the house, travel to the supermarket, load the cart, and, most important, pay the cashier. I'm not going to insult your intelligence by explaining how to shop for groceries at your local supermarket. I'm sure all of you have mastered the art of fruit squeezing, coupon clipping, and comparison shopping by now. So instead of complaining every time you run out of juice or skim milk, why not head to the store and put your shopping skills to good use?

When I came home I expected to have things easy, be on vacation, relax, and have a bunch of free time to do nothing. I'm sure I wasn't always the best person to be around because sometimes I would get very demanding. I remember always getting mad because no one went to buy more cream cheese and I didn't feel like going to get it.

—George, 23, Miami, FL

No matter how understanding your parents are, they're bound to get annoyed every time you complain about running out of cereal. Your best bet is to help out with the grocery shopping whenever possible. If your mom or dad is cooking that night, ask them if they'll need you to pick up anything special for dinner. If you see that a product is running low, make a note of it. Another good rule of thumb is to compose a family shopping list and tack it onto your fridge. That way, you won't forget your parents' favorite items while you're busy stocking up on yours.

Points to ponder:

- Where will the family grocery list be stored? Fridge? Computer?
- How will you contribute financially to buying groceries?
- Who will be responsible for buying what and when?
- If your groceries are going to be separated, where will they be stored?

The Family Wagon

Since some of you will be moving to the suburbs or smaller towns, having a ride will be imperative to getting around. If you've fallen on hard times and can't afford to buy your own car, you're probably going to want to borrow your parents' from time to time. But what if your family only has one car to share? What about insurance, repairs, and gas? Since you'll be borrowing the wheels, shouldn't you be partially responsible for some, if not all, of the above?

The key to sharing the car is to make sure to notify your parents well in advance. You don't want to have a constant battle of wills over who gets the car when. You should also remember to fill it up with gas after using it. You don't want your parents to get stuck on their way to work one day. It might also look good if you washed the old gas-guzzler once in a while with a DIY cleaning job or at your local car wash. A little elbow grease might just win you some extra car privileges.

> When I moved home to the suburbs, one of the biggest challenges was not having my own car. Since the goal was to move out as soon as possible and not have any extra expenditures, I used my parents' car whenever it was available. This put a huge limit on my freedom since I couldn't stay out late in the city during the weekdays because I would have no way of getting home from the train station.
>
> —Cynthia, 23, Long Island, NY

When it comes to car insurance, you'll have to sort out the matter carefully. Unless your parents can add you to their policy or list you as an occassional driver, you may have to purchase your own policy, which means more money down the drain. But even if your parents can add you to their plan, it may cost them extra to do so. Don't forget to ask them how much you're costing them and offer to offset this amount. Even if they refuse to take your money, you'll seem extra considerate for having asked. (Stay tuned for more specific advice on car insurance in Chapter 8.)

Points to ponder:

- How often do you expect to borrow the car?
- Will your car use be limited to day, night, weekends?
- How and when will you notify family members to reserve use of the car?
- How do you plan to contribute to gasoline expenses?
- What about car maintenance and cleaning—who will be responsible?
- Do you plan to contribute to car insurance?

A Wired World

Arguments over who uses the home computer can be draining. Your parents probably have their own Internet connection and may resent you for taking it over. If you're having trouble sharing the connection, try setting up a schedule so everyone has time to check e-mails, shop online, or chat with friends. To prevent hogging, make sure each time slot does not exceed a two-hour period.

> My dad was really annoyed every time I used his home office to check my e-mail or used any of his office supplies. But it's not like I could do anything about it. I couldn't afford a computer of my own and had to use his a lot for job hunting. It became a real sticking point between us.
> —Reanna, 23, Morristown, NJ

Another way to avoid conflict is to go wireless. That way, all of you can be hooked up to the Net at the same time. Your mom can be checking her e-mail while you surf HotJobs.com on your laptop. Not only that, once your laptop is set up to go wireless, you'll be able to get online anywhere there's a hot spot. Most Starbucks coffee shops are now equipped with wireless access (for locations, visit this URL: www.starbucks.com/retail), which means less time at home and more capuccinos for you. Your parents may not be as tech-savvy as you, and will be ultra-impressed that you set this up.

To pull off this technological feat you'll need a wireless router and a wireless card for each computer. For a full tutorial, check out PCmag.com. Don't forget, PC and Apple users will need to invest in different routers and cards. PC users should head to Linksys.com for information; Apple users, to apple.com/airport express to purchase the AirPort router. Still, if your parents have a PC and you can't live without your trusty Mac, AirPort allows you to configure both on one network. So you see? If your Mac and PC computers can live harmoniously under one roof, so can you and your parents.

Points to ponder:

> ➐ Will you have a computer sign-up sheet? If so, where will you store it?
> ➐ Will you contribute to the monthly Internet bill?
> ➐ Who will be responsible for maintaining the computer and work area?
> ➐ Where will you store your personal files on the computer?

Phone Home

Remember the days when only the luckiest kids on the block had their own phone line and three-way calling? Even if your house is still equipped with only one measly line, sharing phone privileges with your parents shouldn't be too complicated. With cell phones so readily available, parents and boomerangers can all breathe a collective sigh of relief. No longer do you have to fight over the phone and argue about lost messages. Having your own cell phone and paying your own bill is really the easiest no-muss, no-fuss solution.

Lest we be insensitive, it's important to note that some of you won't be able to afford your own cell phone and will have no choice but to share your parents' line. Don't worry, there are ways you can do that without strangling each other with the telephone cord. One option is to limit your personal phone calls to about 15 minutes each. Since you're living at home, you're the one who should sacrifice. You should also get in the habit of writing down your parents' messages on a notepad. Stick the note on the fridge just in case you forget to relay the message.

Another bone of contention when it comes to the phone is noise levels. Whether you're on your own cell or tying up the family line, you should be considerate of other household members and keep your voice down whenever possible. Whatever drama you've got going on in your life, your parents don't need to hear about every last detail.

Points to ponder:

- Will you be paying for your part of the phone bill?
- How will you relay messages to your family?
- How long can you use the phone for each conversation?
- Will you be using your cell phone late at night?
- Will you be using your cell phone during dinner?

Music for the Masses

Music can soothe even the most savage boomeranger. Many home-bounders reported using music to cope with the reality of moving back in with the parents. It's totally understandable that you'll want to crank up the tunes whenever the urge strikes. Unfortunately, while some parents and boomerangers have similar taste in music, not all of them share the same undying love for Godsmack, Jay-Z, or the White Stripes.

If the stereo system you're using is in a public area of the house and your parents are in the next room, make sure to ask permission before you turn up the volume. They'll marvel at your consideration and may even agree to listen along with you. If your stereo is located in the privacy of your own room, that doesn't give you carte blanche to blast your music. After all, the walls may be thinner than you think. Turn down the bass *and* the volume so your whole house doesn't shake every time you play a track.

And when in doubt, a personal CD player or iPod is a great way to keep your parents off your back. Not only can you listen to music as loudly as you want, you can also drown out the sound of your dad asking you when you're coming home that night.

Points to ponder:

ꔷ Will you share your family's stereo or invest in a portable music device, like a Discman or an iPod?
ꔷ How loud can you play the household stereo during the day? What about at night?
ꔷ How will you share stereo privileges with the rest of the family?

For Me to Poop On

For all the talk about dogs being a man's best friend, it's ironic how everyone scatters every time the family pooch has to be walked. Taking care of a dog is a huge responsibility. If you're going to be sharing your space with your family pet, it would be a nice gesture if you offered to walk, feed, and clean up after the dog once in a while. When you think about it, walking the dog is one of the best chores, since you're forced to get out of the house and into the fresh air. Believe me, a few days of being cooped up in your old room with nowhere to go but the local 7-Eleven and you'll be grateful for any opportunity to leave the house.

Also, if your parents work full-time, they'll be considerably relieved to have someone on hand to watch the dog. You may even be able to get out of other, more annoying, family chores if you offer to take on canine responsibilities.

Points to ponder:

➐ Who will be responsible for walking, feeding, and cleaning up after the dog?

➐ If the dog gets sick, who will take him/her to the vet?

Guess Who's Not Coming to Dinner?

When I moved home, I was in for a huge surprise. I had no idea the parents and I would be so at odds about everything. I expected them to pretty much leave me alone. They expected me to tell them everything I was doing. The biggest thing was having my boyfriend sleep over in my room. They flat-out refused and told me he would have to sleep on the couch. I was very mad and it got to the point where I just avoided them and tried to keep to myself. If I had known how strict they were going to be about my boyfriend, I may not have been so quick to leave my job and move 100 miles to live at home.

—Heather, 27, Boston, MA

During your free-flying days of living solo, you may have had an open-door policy when it came to visitors. Most of your friends would just stop on by, turning your pad into a social happy hour and eating all your 3-D Doritos. Now that you're living at home, you'll probably miss the good old days. Your parents may not look too kindly on your pals crashing at their place or messing up their house. And who could blame them? Even you have to admit that some of them were freeloaders.

But no worries. Since many of you will be moving to the suburbs, you'll have a heck of a time trying to convince your friends to stay over (unless, of course, there's a pool and hot tub involved). In fact, you may want to cash in on your favors by staying over at *their* places for a change, especially if they live closer to or in the city. At least that way you won't have to bother your parents every time you come home late.

Of course, having a few friends over every now and then shouldn't be too much of an imposition. If some of your pals want to come over, make sure to clear it with your parents in advance. After all, your mom or dad won't appreciate walking out in their bathrobe only to find a group of strangers in the living room.

When it comes to your "special friends" staying over, it's a whole different enchilada. Many parents will find it more than a little bit uncomfortable knowing you're getting busy in the next room (and you should, too, for that matter). This is where some parents pull rank and insist that you not have anyone over or stay at your boyfriend's/girlfriend's place. If you have a steady boyfriend or girlfriend, your parents will probably agree to sleepovers, provided he/she stays in the guest room. Short of taking a vow of celibacy or locking yourself up in the bathroom with porn, you'll need to find other outlets for your love life, like getting hotel rooms (don't laugh, you'd be surprised at what you'll resort to after a month of abstinence) or finding other places to crash.

Points to ponder:

- How many guests can you can invite at any given time?
- How far in advance do your parents need to know about your guest(s) coming over?
- How long can your guest(s) stay during each visit?
- What is the household policy on boyfriend/girlfriend sleepovers?
- What rules of conduct will your guest(s) be responsible for maintaining?

Do Not Disturb

"Can't you see I'm_____ (working, sleeping, talking on phone) here?" Privacy is an important issue for both parents and boomerangers alike. With the kids out of the house, your 'rents have probably gotten used to having their own space and the privacy to do what they want. Of course, the same goes for you. If you've lived in your own apartment for any length of time, you've probably gotten used to walking around in your skivvies. So you probably won't be too thrilled by the prospect of your parents barging into your room and infringing on your rights.

> My biggest problem with living at home is that my mom is always grilling me about what I did today, what I'm planning to do, and where I'm going. I hate having to account for my every move. It feels like I'm living in a reality TV show. I really miss just walking into my apartment and not having to give a full blow-by-blow of my day.
>
> —Paul, 27, New York, NY

As Paul points out, privacy isn't just about personal space. If you haven't already, it's important that you iron out the rules when it comes to reporting to your parents. If you feel that their questions are driving you nuts, make sure to express your feelings in a calm and rational manner. Tell them that you would love to share details about your life, but you'd prefer to volunteer that information rather than constantly be pestered for it.

When it comes to privacy, it's all about mutual respect. You respect your parents' privacy and they respect yours. Make sure your parents know not to pop in unannounced, and make a pointed effort to knock before visiting their room. Also, if you don't want your parents rifling through your personal belongings, explain that your things are strictly off-limits. While you may think this should go without saying, it's better to be explicit about everything and assume nothing.

> For the most part my father respects my privacy, but my mother likes to go through my things. The fact that she thinks she can go through my stuff and tell me that I don't need it drives me crazy. I had this box of old cards from friends and girlfriends and it was sitting there in their house for twenty years. Occasionally I would look through it. But one day I found that half of them were gone. It turned out my mother decided I didn't need them.
>
> —Gus, 35, Hollywood, FL

Points to ponder:

- How will you communicate your need for privacy to each other?
- What are the rules on knocking? Just when the door is closed? Always?
- What are your parents entitled to know about and what are they not?
- Do you prefer to volunteer information about your whereabouts or to be asked?
- What do you and your parents consider to be an invasion of privacy?
- Is your room off-limits to parents when you are away?

Lights Out

It's bad enough that we have to give up some freedoms by coming home, but dare we even utter the word "curfew"? The mere mention is enough to send us over the edge. Curfew is often a huge sticking point for many boomerangers and parents. That's because the word itself reminds us of a time when we had no say in or control over our own lives. It may seem completely barbaric to have a curfew at this point in your life. After all, you've been on your own forever. It might even feel like your parents are trying to kick you when you're down. You're old enough to decide when to come home, right?

Some parents wouldn't dream of setting a curfew, feeling that they can trust you to return at a decent hour and not disrupt the entire household as you stumble through the door. However, there are parents who won't look too kindly on you staying out past three every night. Whether or not your righteous indignation is justified, you'll have to iron out an arrangement that everyone can live with.

Don't discount the notion that while many of us boomerangers are holding down jobs, contributing to the household, and being responsible adults, there are others who would benefit from some structure in their lives. If you're not doing much all day and partying all night, it would be unfair to expect your parents to just sit by and watch as you throw your life down the drain. When it comes to curfew, it really should be established on a case-by-case basis.

If your parents want to impose a lights-out policy, make sure that it's something both of you can agree on. If it's a matter of you coming home before a certain hour because they have to wake up in the morning for work, try to accommodate them. But then request that they be lenient when it comes to weekends. Worse comes to worse, arrange to stay at a friend's house when you want to pull an all-nighter. Who knows? They may even agree to a courtesy call if you're going to be out too late. In which case, make sure to call on time so that your hard-won privileges don't get revoked.

Points to ponder:

- What is the household curfew during the week and weekends?
- What are the consequences of breaking curfew?
- Are there other alternatives to having a curfew: phoning in, sleeping at a friend's house, etc.?
- If phoning in works for them, what is the latest you can call on weekends and weeknights?

Purple Haze

There's a big difference between being a crack addict and having a beer with dinner. Of course, some parents, especially of the Mormon variety, will not approve of anything even remotely resembling foreign substances.

Being that most of you are of legal drinking and smoking age, what you do on your own time is really your own business. However, and this is a big HOWEVER, if your parents are against drinking in their house and don't even indulge in the occasional spirit, it's not exactly polite to pull up a kegger and start chugging beer on the front lawn. No matter how restrictive their attitude, you have to respect where they're coming from. Of course, that doesn't mean you can't indulge by going to the local bar or maybe even establishing a parental-approved drinking zone, like the backyard, basement, or some other out-of-the-way area.

My parents pretty much had a "don't ask / don't tell" policy when it came to anything going on outside their house. But

The same goes for you nicotine fiends out there. No matter how much you loved rolling out of bed and taking a puff off your first morning cigarette, you may not be able to indulge quite so readily. For those smokers moving back to a smoke-free dwelling, prepare to make some major concessions. Of course, you could always take this opportunity as a sign to quit. But if that's not an option, take it outside. That way your parents won't be nagging you every time you light up, and you can get away for a much-needed moment of peace and quiet.

Another sensitive subject and one that shouldn't be taken too lightly is drug use. Boomerangers should be aware that smoking pot or anything else in the house is really not fair to your parents. Not only are they legally responsible for whatever drugs you're bringing into the house, being stoned all day is not exactly the best strategy for getting your life together. No matter how clueless you think your parents are, they'll eventually figure out what's going on. And when that happens, prepare for some serious battles ahead.

Points to ponder:

- What is the drinking policy in the house?
- What is the smoking policy in the house?
- Are there any designated areas in the house for smoking or drinking?
- Will your guests be allowed to smoke or drink in the house?
- What are the consequences of breaking these rules?

Rugrats

If little kids are in the picture, you'll need a host of rules to keep the peace in your house. After all, the fuller the nest, the bigger the issues. Your first order of business is to address basic concerns like child care, discipline, and safety. If you're planning to work during the day and need one of your parents to watch your kids, make sure to clear that in advance. Outline just how much child care you will require of your family members, and try to be as honest in that estimate as possible. Parents don't want to be treated like babysitters, and may resent it if you spring watching the kids on them at the last minute. So make sure to alert them well in advance if you're planning to go out and leave the kids in their care.

When it comes to setting guidelines for your kids, spelling it out clearly is the best way to go. You should write out everything so both you and your parents understand what is and is not acceptable. Make sure to include a full list of guidelines about eating, entertainment, playing, and sleeping so there is no confusion.

The issue of discipline is also a major consideration. If you're planning on working full-time, you'll need to set rules for how and when your children will be disciplined. Talk to your parents about your child-rearing philosophy so they know what's expected of them. The last thing you want to do is send your children mixed messages. If Mommy doesn't like the kids to snack on sugary sweets or watch TV after school and Grandma says it's okay, your kids will have a hard time identifying the key decision maker/disciplinarian.

In all this talk of snacking and TV habits, let's not forget to mention that kids can be a major financial drain. If you are planning to return home with children in tow, make a concerted effort to contribute what you can, whether it's for groceries, household repair, or cleaning supplies.

Points to ponder:

- Who will take care of the kids when you are at work or away?
- How long in advance do you need to notify your parents if you are planning to go away?
- What type of discipline have you approved for your children?
- What are some rules and child-rearing guidelines that you adhere to?
- Who will be responsible for transporting kids to school, day care, lessons, sports, etc.?

Tenant Beware

Besides figuring out how long you'll stay (a subject we'll discuss in the next section), determining your rent or household financial contribution will be one of the most important tasks ahead of you. Of course, with about 60 percent of adult children who return home not paying any rent at all, many of you are probably wondering why you should have to contribute.

Contrary to popular belief, living rent-free is not the nirvana-like experience most boomerangers will have you believe. When it comes to living at home, there's really no such thing as a free lunch, free dinner, or a free anything for that matter. No matter what you think you're saving in dollars, you'll have to make up for it at some point—in fights, headaches, and plenty of recriminations.

Take Ken, for example. When he returned to the family nest, he thought he was going to be cruising on easy street—until the full reality of his situation finally dawned on him.

> My parents were really cool about not asking for rent. That was one of the reasons I decided to move home. At first we got along great. But after a few months, I could tell I was beginning to grate on their nerves. My mom and dad began picking at little things, like how I left my cereal bowl on the kitchen table every morning or that I left my bed unmade every day. Finally, we sat down and talked about the issues and it came out that they were a bit miffed with me for not helping out at all. If I had known they would have been so upset, I would have paid them a bit each month, which is what I decided to do. Now I pay them $150 a month for rent, groceries, and all the extras. I also try to pitch in on cleaning and stuff. It's a small price to pay, especially since they were so much easier to get along with after the talk.
>
> —Ken, 32, Phoenix, AZ

Sometimes the more you contribute, the more freedom you'll be able to buy yourself. Not only that, if your parents tend to treat you like a child, paying even a small amount of rent can show them you're ready to be taken seriously. When it comes to being treated like an equal, money really does talk.

And with all that cash you're laying out, think about how motivated you'll be to get a job, even if it's a part-time gig to get you through the month. Part of what makes us so apathetic and lazy at home is the idea that there's no accountability or consequences to

I know, I know, it seems a little absurd to pay rent or household bills when the whole point of moving home is to save money. After all, if you're going to be making such a huge sacrifice to live at home, the least your parents can do is to comp the whole thing, right? Wrong! Don't underestimate the power of paying your own way. Even if your parents make a trillion times more than you do and you're completely brokesters, a little bit goes a long way. In fact, before you even move in, present your parents with these four payment plans (or at least one you can actually afford).

Basic Package
$50 rent
1 chore per week

Silver Package
$150 rent
1 household bill
3 hours of cleanup per week

Gold Package
$300 rent
1 household bill
3 home-cooked meals
2 trips to the grocery store

Platinum Package
$500 rent
2 household bills
2 loads of family laundry per
    week
Weekly lawn mowing

our actions. By having to pay rent each month, you'll be giving yourself a reason to get out of bed every morning.

Even if your parents refuse to take a penny from you, figure out a way to contribute somehow. Whether it's by taking on more household chores, assuming kitchen duty, or taking responsibility for the family pet, there are many ways for you to help. Some parents who accept rent have been known to save those checks and deposit them into their boomeranger's savings account or into a CD. That way they can allay their parental guilt about taking money from their kids while fostering a sense of responsibility.

Points to ponder:

➐ How much will you contribute toward rent?
➐ When will rent be paid every month?
➐ What household bills, if any, will you cover?

If you are currently unemployed, will the amount of your rent increase once you have found a job?

Length of Stay

Since most guests wear out their welcome in a matter of days, consider yourself lucky to be able to crash as long as you have. And how long exactly *are* you planning to stay? Didn't quite get around to figuring that out, did you? You can't expect your parents to keep the welcome mat out indefinitely. Even if you have no idea when you're moving out, it's never too late to set a departure date. In fact, the sooner you set a firm deadline, the easier both you and your parents can breathe.

For anyone who thinks that setting a departure date is a waste of time, consider the fact that most problems at home stem from misunderstandings about this very issue. The boomeranger moves in, the parents assume it will only be for a couple of months, and when he/she doesn't leave after that, the parents find themselves becoming more and more irate. Most parents have no idea how to broach the issue, thinking themselves to be heartless ogres if they even hint at kicking you out.

> I figured I would eventually move out. But then a couple of months turned into a couple of years, and soon I was 28 years old and still living at home. I wanted to save money, but I ended spending most of it on dinners and clubs in the city. After two years at home, I was really no closer to reaching any of my goals and my parents were getting more and more annoyed with me since my staying at home prevented them from selling the house and moving into a smaller one.
>
> —Lisa, 29, Lake Forest, IL

The last thing you want to do is interfere with your parents' hopes for retirement, relocation, and peace and quiet. And while some parents will want to get you out of the house as soon as possible, setting a move-out date can also help you deal with parents who would rather keep you at home indefinitely. Whether your parent is ailing, widowed, or divorced, many boomerangers find themselves locked into living at home with no definite end in sight. Having arrived to help a parent deal with a life trauma or transition, they find that as time goes on, it gets harder and harder to leave. By setting a firm deadline and discussing it with your parents, you'll be able to avoid any unnecessary guilt trips and arguments once you're ready to move out on your own again.

But don't think setting a deadline is just for your parents' peace of mind. It's just as important for you. Without a clear goal or time limit, it's very tempting to defer looking for a job, saving money, and finding a new place to live. In fact, boomerangers who fail to draft a move-out timeline are less motivated and are much more likely to stay home longer.

When setting a date, it's important to be realistic about your financial, professional, educational, and emotional goals. If you set a date that's too soon, you may feel pressured to meet the deadline. If your date is too far in the future, you may not feel enough impetus to make things happen and may put off fulfilling your objectives until a later day. Here are some guidelines that will help you set just the right time frame for your stay at home.

Financial Goals. If you moved home in order to save money for a house, pay down your credit card/school loan, or to create a nest egg, you'll need to figure out how much money you can save each month. Once you have a number in mind, do the math ($500 × 12 months = $6,000 per year). Determine how much you'll need to stash in order to feel comfortable, and then calculate how many months or years it will take you to meet that goal. It's important that you show your parents the breakdown so they understand how much time you'll need at home.

Professional Goals. Since many of you return home because you're sick of your jobs and are looking to make a career transition or start a small business, it's important that you give yourselves plenty of time to get things rolling. If you're making a career transition, give yourself six months to one year in order to fully analyze your options, network within your chosen industry, and ultimately land a good job in your new field. If starting a small business is on your agenda, make sure to outline a strict timeline for the launch. Have a deadline for every goal, whether it's drafting a business plan, securing financing, or marketing your services. Try not to stay at home for more than two years, since it may not put enough pressure on you to get the business up and running.

Educational Goals. If you're planning to return home to attend graduate school, it's important to figure in not only the amount of time you'll be in school, but also how long you'll need to land a job once you graduate. If you're attending a two-year master's program, you'll probably stay home for at least six months after the completion date. And if you're planning to pursue a Ph.D., you may have to stay far longer. Not only will you have a large school loan to pay down, you'll find that the job search may take longer than you expected. By discussing all these contingencies with your parents, they won't be surprised when you don't move out the same day you're handed a diploma.

Emotional/Personal Goals. Many young adults move home after a life setback, relationship problem, or psychological issue like addiction and depression. For those of you moving home to regroup and strengthen yourself after a traumatic or emotionally taxing event, you'll need to be extra vigilant about setting a deadline. On one hand, no one can predict the length of your individual healing process. While it would be nice to recover overnight, it often takes longer than we think. On the other hand, if you stay too long and wallow in whatever misery brought you to your family's doorstep, you may get caught up in a vicious circle without any definite ending in sight. If you are moving home for emotional reasons, make sure you set up a timeline and schedule activities that will help you get past your problems. Whether it's starting therapy, joining a support group, or just doing something you love every day, you'll need to have a concrete plan for getting back on your feet.

BEDROOM REHAB

After about two years of living in my old room, I slowly found myself going nuts. I never planned to be there that long, so I hadn't done a thing to it. The room had the same crappy furniture and my old pink comforter with flowers on it. One day, I just exploded and boxed everything up that was old and threw it in the attic. I then repainted all the walls, hung up new artwork, and bought new curtains and a comforter. It was tough getting around to it, but I knew I couldn't have taken another year in that room.

—Elaine, 26, Sarasota, FL

Being in perpetual denial is a trait shared by most boomerangers. We're always battling the idea of permanence, telling ourselves that it's only for a few months. So even though many of us will end up staying far longer, we rarely get around to fixing up our rooms. On one hand, decorating your old room is a sign that you're putting down roots. No matter how much you've tried to deny it up to this point, sprucing up your digs is a full-on admission of your boomeranger status. On the other hand, if you don't do something about all those plush toys, soccer trophies, and old *Curious George* books, any shreds of adulthood you may have salvaged may disappear entirely. That's right, it's a simple case of damned if you do, damned if you don't. Of course, if you're going to be damned, you may as well do it in style and comfort.

Part of what will make your transition home easier is to inject your new self into your old life. And what better way to start than in the place you'll be calling home for a while—your old bedroom? Even if you luck out and make your grand exit after only a few months, why not leave a well-decorated and organized room as a reminder of your presence? Regardless of how long you're planning to crash at home—six months, one year, three years or more—you should make an effort to spruce up your environment and get organized at the outset. Not only will it make your time at home more productive, serene, and enjoyable, it will show your parents that you have clearly outgrown your old Cabbage Patch collection. One quick tip: Don't forget to clue your parents in on your decorating plans. While most parents would be more than glad to give you free rein, others may not want you messing up their color palette.

Get Organized

Before you craft your plan of attack, whether it's finding a new job, putting together your photography portfolio, or starting a business, you'll need to get organized. The key to working efficiently out of your bedroom, basement, or attic is to keep all your papers and belongings neatly sorted. Since you probably have all your new and old belongings cluttering your space, organizing everything can be one tough task. And if your parents have been using your old room as storage, that will make sorting and cleaning doubly difficult. But have no fear; whatever your situation, following these simple steps will get you organized in no time.

1. Set a Time. In order to get a grip on all that clutter, you'll need to schedule a day or even a weekend during which you will devote all your time to cleaning, sorting, and piling. Make sure to inform everyone of your plans so you don't get interrupted. Once you've scheduled a date, make sure to keep it.

2. Give It Up. Before you get down to business, you'll need to get three boxes. The first should be labeled "Donate," the second "Sell," and the third labeled "Dump." Once you've got your three boxes ready, go through all your clothes, memorabilia, and other assorted items and decide where each belongs. If you have items in good condition, you may want to place them in the "donate" or "sell" piles. But if something looks beyond repair or doesn't have any value, you might want to toss it. If you're worried you may get too sentimental (and you might very well after going through all your stuff past and present), ask a trusted friend or relative to help you with the process. After all, they may not have the same emotional attachment and can help you discard unnecessary items when you're feeling stuck.

3. Assign a Home. Once you've eliminated all the extras and are down to the bare necessities, you'll need to find a home for every item. If you're having trouble finding a place for each item, it may be time to add more storage to your room. You can add drawers under your bed or an extra rod in your closet for clothes. Insufficient or inadequate storage is the number one source of clutter, so head to your local department store (or dollar store if you're on a budget) and invest in some extra crates, shoe racks, and bins pronto!

4. Sort Your Papers. Getting a handle on your important papers—including tax documents, insurance applications, letters, bills, and bank statements—will keep you from freaking out every time you walk into your room. It's very hard to work at your desk when you can't even find it. Since you're in a transient state and don't know where you'll be in a few months, your best bet is a portable filing system that can be easily transported from place to place or hung on your wall. You should also consider buying a rolling filing cabinet or caddy so you can move your paperwork from room to room.

Decorating on a Dime

Now that all your stuff is neatly put away, you'll need to make sure your space looks good, too. It's completely understandable if some of you have little to no motivation to redesign your old room. There's also the problem of not having enough money. Since some of you will be between jobs or looking to save rather than spend what little cash you do have, you'll need to find affordable ways to transform your childhood bedroom into an adult space.

Color You Pretty. Painting your room is the fastest and cheapest way to turn a drab interior into a warm environment. For about $10 to $20 per gallon, you can cover up all the finger painting and wall scrawling you did as a child. Choose colors like terra cotta, mustard, and tans for a more vibrant and inviting look. Or try light greens, blues, or purples for a cooler feel.

Bargain Basement. Flea markets, garage sales, and eBay are virtual treasure troves of undiscovered gems. The key is to use your imagination to convert old, dilapidated pieces into funky, contemporary pieces. So get creative! If you're looking for a comfy armchair, don't feel that you have to splurge on something new. Instead, look for a chair with a great shape and use a bright slipcover to hide the dated upholstery. Or, if you find a great dresser that's a little tattered and worn, don't let it just sit there collecting dust. Try painting it white and replacing the knobs for a shabby chic look that would cost you hundreds at the store.

If you can't be bothered to scrounge around in old musty basements and flea markets, all is not lost. There's plenty of new furniture to be had for bargain-basement prices. Check out these stores for sweet furniture deals that won't break the bank.

- Target (www.target.com)
- Ikea (www.ikea.com)
- Urban Outfitters (www.urbanoutfitters.com) (not so much for house stuff)
- Overstock (www.overstock.com)

Rearrange Your Furniture. You'd be surprised how different your room can look if you just move your furniture around a bit. Not only can it be a huge space saver, you'll also feel as if you've just moved into a whole new place. You should first start by moving the largest item in your room, your bed. See if you can tilt it an angle or move it to the opposite side of the room. If your dresser is taking up a lot of space, try moving it into your closet or a corner to make it look less conspicuous. A few minor changes here and there and pretty soon you won't even recognize your old room.

It's All in the Details. If you're pinching pennies but still want to give your room a face-lift, think about adding some decorative details. Area rugs in bright, bold colors and patterns can take a room from drab to dynamic in seconds. Vases, candle holders, and mirrors can liven up blank wall space and give you something to look at as you plan your next move. You should also consider replacing your old posters with framed prints that inspire you. And finally, don't forget the bedspread, pillows, and curtains. To save some money on these items, head on over to your local fabric store and make them yourself.

5

GET OVER IT!
BATTLING THE DARK SIDE

Since I've been living at home, I've had mixed feelings—depressed because I feel stuck at home and I can't support myself yet, but sometimes happy to be able to have had the chance to improve my relationship with my parents. For me, living at home with them is a sign of my lack of independence. I feel that I am definitely less ambitious and motivated than most of my independent-living peers. I feel that I have it easy, with my parents supporting me, so I don't have to work as hard, or if I'm in a job that I don't like, I can leave, knowing that I would still be taken care of. I feel that I am on the brink of becoming an adult, and what will get me there is living on my own. I still feel like a child, and my parents do baby me sometimes, but mostly the challenges are internal. I thought by the time I turned 27, I would be on my own. It feels pretty crappy that I'm not.

—Carey, 27, New York, NY

Sob stories are a dime a dozen. Everyone has one. But is there anything worse than a bunch of boomerangers whining about their lot in life? Probably not. And besides, there's probably a million people who are worse off than we are. What with homelessness, war, the threat of terrorism, and world hunger, shouldn't we be grateful for what we have? Even if we can't call it our own, at least we have a roof over our heads.

Sure, it's silly to feel sorry for ourselves—we all know that. But now that we've gotten that out of our system, let's take a moment to do just that. What's so wrong with feeling sorry for ourselves, anyway? Even if our problems aren't huge in comparison to all the atrocities going on in the world, they are, after all, *our* problems. However minuscule they seem in the big scheme of things, our problems are still big to us.

To be fair, boomerangers are hardly the most downtrodden members of our population. Most of the time our lives are pretty okay; we have food on the table and our parents' digital cable to keep us entertained. But since this is *your* book and its sole purpose is to edify, simplify, and generally fortify your life, you're entitled to a little indulgence. So before we continue, let's acknowledge one thing: Moving back home with your parents can be tough, and don't let anyone tell you otherwise.

Panic, shame, depression, confusion, and regression: these are just some of the many nasty emotions that you'll have to battle on a daily basis. Whether you're excited or traumatized by the prospect of moving back home, you're bound to feel weird and unsettled at some point during your stay. The key is to remember that no matter what you're going through, others have been there and survived it.

This chapter will discuss some of the biggest emotional and psychological traps we set for ourselves, and will provide practical tips from boomerangers who have grappled with the very same issues that are keeping you up at night. And just so you can continue focusing on the bright side, you'll also find a guide outlining some of the hidden benefits of moving back home. But whatever you take away from this chapter, make sure you don't forget these three simple truths:

1. You're not alone.
2. You're not weird.
3. And no, you're not going crazy!

THE BIG BOOMERANG TRAPS

Trap 1. The Panic Room

A couple of weeks before my big move back home, I started having recurring nightmares. I dreamt that I was in a long tunnel with a huge metal door at the end. I kept trying to get to the door, walking quickly to open it. But the closer I got, the farther the door receded. Finally, I started running and hyperventilating. There was just no end in sight. I guess I don't need a shrink to interpret such a clear-cut dream. I was terrified that once I moved home, I would be trapped for good. It happened once before, when I moved home right after college. Back then, I got so used to the sense of comfort and security that it completely paralyzed my resolve and determination to get out on my own.

—Sandra, 28, Louisville, KY

Upon first arriving on your family's doorstep, you may have been brimming with excitement. The prospect of moving home and starting over may have led you to make lots of resolutions, like taking acting classes, finishing that great American novel you've been bragging about, or maybe even breaking into a new field like public relations or event planning. Many of you thought it would be as simple as taking a few months to bond with the family, de-stress, figure out a new life direction, and then move out on your own again.

Fast-forward one year later: You're still at home. You're exhausted from doing nothing all day, have yet to find a job even after sending out hundreds of resumes, and are fighting constantly with your parents. That's when the panic sets in. You start pacing around the house like a caged animal, talking to yourself, wondering how you ever got yourself into this mess. You start coming up with all kinds of escape plans—joining the Peace Corps for a year, traveling with the Hare Krishnas, going to Hollywood to pursue a career as a butt double—anything and everything to get out of there. But the longer you stay at home, the more you begin to worry that you may never leave, find a job, or become a full-fledged adult.

Don't worry. Panic will come and go. The problem is you never know when it will strike. That's why it's important to avoid making decisions while you're in a state of anxiety. We all experience moments when we worry that we will spend the rest of our lives at home. The trick is not to lose perspective and to remember that this, too, shall pass. Here's some advice from boomerangers who've been there and gotten over that.

Elina's Remedy: Realize that feeling trapped doesn't just happen to you when you're living at home with your parents. It can happen anywhere, anytime—at your job, in a relationship, even with your friends. When you start getting panicky, don't be afraid to confront your anxiety. Reason with yourself: Panic is just a feeling and cannot physically harm you in any way. After a while, you'll feel capable of handling and mastering any anxiety attacks.

Tom's Remedy: What I used to do, and this works really well, was to just keep reminding myself that it's only temporary. Whenever I freaked out or got into a fight with my mom, I would just go to my room, take deep breaths, and outline all my goals and plans for the future. Then I would blast my stereo or TV to distract myself. Sometimes I would even jump around the room to get rid of all the extra energy.

Lauren's Remedy: Since a lot of my friends were working full-time and didn't have the patience to deal with my "episodes," I formed a support group of people living at home. I found them online, through friends, and through recommendations. We were from all over the country and extremely different in our own ways. It was really great. Every time one of us was upset, we would just call each other and talk it through. I can't tell you how many times I called these people. It really helped to have someone to talk to.

Trap 2. Your Dirty Little Secret

> I hate to admit this but one of the major reasons it took me so long to move home was because I worried that no decent guy would ever date me. I figured why would anyone want to date someone who is a mama's girl and immature. I was so freaked out about what guys would think about me that I didn't even stop to think that living with my parents was in my best interest. I just couldn't deal with going out and having to be embarrassed every time someone asked me where I lived. Finally, one of my male friends told me I was being crazy and that my insecurity was more of a turnoff than living at home could ever be.
> —Lisa, 24, Phoenix, AZ

While some of us may have gotten over the initial embarrassment of living with parents, there are many more that are secretly harboring feelings of shame. Many of us ask, is it appropriate to still be living at home? Is it wrong to live at home after 25, after 30, after 40? We look to others to tell us what's okay because deep down we still worry that our living situation is somehow abnormal. So while the stigma of moving home has been diminished greatly, insecurities about our own personal development and maturity levels still plague us from time to time.

> I definitely was chastised by some of my peers for still living with my parents at that point, and adults were even worse about it. The smug "oh, you're still living at home" that I did get from quite a few people when asked about my current situation and future plans was very annoying.
> —Amy, 26, Ballston Lake, NY

Shame is a terrible emotion. No one likes to feel ashamed, so we rarely admit to feeling that way to ourselves or anyone else for that matter. We're so quick to defend ourselves, telling everyone in earshot that living at home is the sensible decision and that we'll be better off financially than all our friends. What's a few years at home if it means saving tons of cash to buy a new car, start our own business, or put a down payment on a condo?

While all this sounds well and good, there's a part of us that wonders if we're not just full of hot air. When our friends go back to their bachelor/bachelorette pads after a night of partying and we go to our parents' house, there's this nagging, persistent voice in our heads whispering, "Something is wrong." Despite all the evidence to the contrary, like your friend just wasting half his month's salary on a new PlayStation and flat screen TV, we often wonder if somehow we aren't less capable, less mature, and less together than our independently dwelling peers. No matter how much we try to avoid it, it's important to admit that being a little mortified with our lot in life comes with the territory. It's not rational and it's not right—but there you have it.

Elina's Remedy: It's okay to feel embarrassed. The one thing worse than being ashamed is to feel ashamed about feeling ashamed. That's one double whammy you don't want to deal with. So before you do irreparable damage to your self-esteem, admit to your feelings. No matter how great your mom is, no matter how much privacy the basement provides, no matter how many of your friends are in the same boat, you're still a wee bit weirded out about living at home. Now doesn't that feel better?

David's Remedy: I felt completely judged by peers and acquaintances. The first question they would ask was, "So, where do you live now? I just got an apartment." They'd expect me to respond with a similar answer and were surprised that I am still at home. I have to admit that it made me feel kind of iffy about myself. But I refused to get down about things and really focused on what I had going in my life, like traveling and going on vacation. Because I was saving so much money, I was able to take many more vacations than my friends. I guess that helped me get over some of those issues.

Emily's Remedy: I kind of felt like I was to blame for ending up at home, that I didn't make the right contacts, get the right job, or do anything right for that matter. Funny thing was, my parents and little sister all looked up to me because I had lived in a big city for two years. They were always in awe of these ridiculous little things, like when I introduced them to buying stamps online or decorated my room on a tiny budget by scouring local flea markets. They also loved to listen to all my stories about all the fun celebrity parties I've been to. Their positive reactions really boosted my confidence and helped me realize how much I had going for me.

Trap 3. Slacker Nation

I felt depressed moving back home. I had lived in my home 18 years until departing for school and moving on with my life. After four years of school, it was a huge letdown to revert back to my old situation. I felt almost like I had been treading water the whole time. It's great seeing the parents but there is a time in everyone's life to move on, which can be quite frustrating if you can't. I feel less successful since I haven't jumped into my next life stage.

—Kyle, 26, Philadelphia, PA

Unmotivated, depressed, and listless—these are just some of the most common complaints parents have about their boomeranger. The stereotype of the deadbeat, slacker kid who spends most of his/her time eating the family out of house and home, watching too much television, and sleeping well into the afternoon is a sad but often true reality.

While many boomerangers would never dream of losing sight of their goals and moping around the house in their jammies all day, many do in fact find themselves battling depression and apathy as they struggle to make sense of their lives. What's even more ironic is that many of these same boomerangers were once shiny, happy people who looked forward to the idea of going home to recuperate. What starts out as a short break from the hassles of everyday life can often turn into a protracted stay with no definite end in sight.

Not only is the slacker mentality harmful to the boomerangers themselves, it can also create a severe rift in the family. It's not unusual for parents to get upset that their previously ambitious offspring is now devoid of goals or motivation. Parents who feel that they're bending over backward to help don't appreciate feeling as if they're being taken advantage of, especially when the dishes get piled in the sink, the laundry goes unwashed, and the groceries never get restocked. Frustrated but at a loss as to what to do, parents often react by placing additional stress on the boomeranger at a time when they should be the most supportive.

If you're taking up residence in your old room in the 'burbs, are financially and emotionally distressed, and have no game plan in place, you may eventually come to experience feelings of worthlessness, lethargy, and depression. So how do you cope and where do you turn for help? As grim as this picture looks, there's always a way out.

I was extremely motivated when I moved back home. I sent out dozens of resumes and tried to network. The first month, I was on a roll. I had three interviews. I was sure something would come out of it. But when I didn't get hired by any of the companies, it was a serious blow to my ego. Slowly, the calls started trickling in less and less. Five months later, I could barely bring myself to write a cover letter. I just felt that I was setting myself up for another failure. It didn't help that my parents thought I was slacking with my job search. The more they started pressuring me, the more depressed I became about the whole thing.

—Adam, 24, Sarasota, FL

Elina's Remedy: Your first step is to determine whether your lack of motivation is a sign of a deeper issue. There's a big difference between needing a kick in the pants every now and then and being clinically depressed. If it's just your run of the mill dissatisfaction you should make an effort to acknowledge and validate your feelings. It's completely normal to feel depressed and concerned about where you're headed. Your life may not have worked out the way you planned, but how often does everything go according to plan? There is a profound truth in the saying, "If you want God to laugh, tell him your plans." Just imagine the alternative. What if you were satisfied with your life by the time you turned 30? Nothing else to strive for, no challenges to overcome, no ventures to look forward to—that could be really terrifying. As humans we all have a propensity to get complacent and smug. That's why at every stage of our life we're presented with new challenges to overcome, new risks to take, and new heights to reach. So when things get rough, just remember—this may be one of those times.

Doug's Remedy: I've always needed a lot of structure in my life. So when I was out of work and living at home, everything fell apart. There was no point in getting up early in the morning and no point in getting dressed. So I turned into a complete slob. Finally, I decided that I needed to set my own schedule. Once I crafted what seemed to be a workable routine, I followed it very carefully. I woke up at the same time each day as if I were going to work, showered, and even got dressed to go out. I would also have dinner at the same time every night and go to sleep at around midnight, just to get myself into a routine. I would also avoid answering the phone from noon to four every day, so I could concentrate on my job search.

Jessica's Remedy: My game plan was that as soon as I got a full-time job, I was going to move out. I didn't set a timeline, but I knew I had to move out within a few months. I felt that I was just as driven if not more so than my independent-living peers because I was looking for a job on a daily basis. I was really looking forward to having a place of my own so I was even more determined. Living at home isn't always the best, but you have to admit, it can be a great incentive for getting your life together.

Top Signs You May Need Professional Help

We all get confused, frustrated, and depressed from time to time. It's not unusual to feel all those things in the span of one week or even one day. But if you're trying to get over a major setback like getting fired or divorced, or overcoming an addiction, you need to be extra vigilant when it comes to your mood swings. If you do find that you're experiencing three or more of the following signs, you should see a professional counselor regardless of the time commitment or cost.

- You feel consistently sad, anxious, or empty.
- Feelings of hopelessness and pessimism plague you on a daily basis.
- Your sleeping habits have changed; you're sleeping either more or less often.
- You experience feelings of guilt, worthlessness, and helplessness.
- You have lost interest in old hobbies and activities that you once enjoyed.
- You feel more lethargic and not as energized as before.
- You have difficulty staying focused and concentrating, are easily distracted, and agonize over every decision.
- You've lost or gained more than ten pounds in the past few months.
- You are preoccupied with thoughts of death and suicide.
- You are easily annoyed and irritable.

Need help? Contact the National Institute of Mental Health for more information. Phone: 301-443-4513. Web: www.nimh.nih.gov

Trap 4. Lost in Transition

> I always thought I was going to be a lawyer. I had it all planned out—the color of my convertible Mercedes, the ring tone on my cell phone, and my entire professional wardrobe. I was going to be the most successful lawyer ever. I thought it was what I wanted, but when it came down to enrolling in law school, I couldn't do it. By then, I had heard a lot of stories about unhappy lawyers billing themselves into an early grave. I just couldn't deal with four years of school followed by 30 more years of overworking myself. Problem was, I never entertained any other options. I hoped moving in with my parents would buy me some time while I came up with another plan.
>
> —Sarah, 24, Chicago, IL

Once college is over, the rest of our lives just kind of looms there, hovering all around us like a giant, shapeless blob.

"The rest of your life."

"The rest of your life."

Not at all daunting, is it? These words conjure up the same feeling one gets when sitting in front of a blank computer screen. The idea that there are so many words and a million ways to arrange them is enough to drive anyone into a serious case of writer's block—or, in your case, a life block.

With so many options available, some of us didn't bother to iron out every last detail of our future. We figured that at some point the answers would just come to us, that one day we'd wake up and have it all figured out. And even if we did manage to plan everything out like Sarah, it's very rare that life events unfold according to some half-baked plan we hatched in high school.

Second-guessing every decision has become a common scenario. Think about how many sleepless nights you've spent tossing and turning as you weighed all the pros and cons of Plan A or Plan B. Is it any wonder we often lose confidence in the face of so much uncertainty?

Meanwhile, living at our parents' seems like a no-brainer. After all, it seems like a waste to shell out all our hard-earned cash to a slumlord while we're trying to sort thing out. Who needs the extra financial pressure while we're dealing with the strain of getting our lives together?

Problem is, very rarely does everything become crystal clear over a year's time. When the epiphany that we hoped for doesn't come on schedule, we tend to slide deeper into a fog of confusion. And it doesn't help that we become so comfortable that finding a goal becomes secondary to getting home in time for dinner. A few months turns into a year. A year turns into two, and pretty soon, it's eight years later and we're still no closer to figuring out what we want to do with our lives.

Elina's Remedy: Now that you're a free agent, it's important that you explore all your options. Remember those times in your cubicle when you fantasized about what you would do if you weren't chained to your desk? So what's stopping you now? Take that creative writing class, for crying out loud, find a low-cost art class in your area, learn to meditate, or volunteer a few hours each week at an animal shelter. You never know when and where inspiration will strike. It's harder to find answers when you're always looking for them. So by getting out there, distracting yourself, and doing the things you enjoy, you will be closer to finding what truly fulfills you.

Jessica's Remedy: It's important to avoid the all-or-nothing mentality. Instead of thinking about what would make you happy in the long run, focus on what would make you happy right now. I worried every decision and second-guessed myself at every turn. I'd wonder if I would be happy being a jewelry designer when I'm 50 or if I could see myself being an interior decorator for the next 30 years? I finally had to stop since I was driving myself crazy. I replaced those questions with: What hobbies make me happy? What do I do that makes me feel like time is standing still? Once I answered those questions, it made it much easier to decide on a new course. And, besides, isn't it common to change careers and direction every few years? How many of us really know where we'll be in five years?

Kyle's Remedy: I hated having no goals or purpose, especially with my parents and friends pressuring me to get on with my life and do something. I found myself getting really bored, depressed, and wasting my days watching television. One day, after a particularly boring episode of *Crossing Over with John Edward*, I went to my room and made a list of all the things I wanted to do before I turned 30. As soon as I started writing, my mood improved. Since then I've

---

Six Surefire Strategies for Staying Motivated

It's easy to lose track of your goals when you're living in a pressure-free zone at home. All that cable, Internet access, and time on your hands can be a recipe for disaster. The key to success is to prepare yourself and to have a game plan for avoiding inertia. Here are some tried-and-true strategies for keeping yourself motivated.

1. *Reflect on your life purpose.* Do you contribute to society? Do you change or improve people's lives? Does this give you fulfillment and satisfaction? Take time each day to think about what you're doing and whether it's in alignment with your bigger life goals. Focusing and visualizing yourself doing what you love most is the surest way to get where you want to be.
2. *Read or watch biographies.* It's not easy to be inspired day in and day out. In fact, looking around at all the grumpy nine-to-fivers, you'd be hard-pressed to want to emulate them. Successful people like writers, dancers, entrepreneurs, even politicians have captivating stories and are a great source of inspiration. Whether you'd prefer reading or watching shows like VH-1's *Driven* or the Biography Channel, there's always a lesson, a formula, or a pattern to be learned from every rags-to-riches story. So pay attention and maybe you'll crack the secret code.
3. *Do at least three things every day.* Whether it's making a phone call or writing a letter, make sure you do three small things to further your agenda each day. That way you won't lose momentum and will keep moving toward your final destination.
4. *Complete your toughest task first.* Start each day by listing your top three to five most important to-dos for the day. Arrange them in order from "toughest" to "easiest." Do the toughest first and the rest of your day will seem like a breeze in comparison.

5. *Organize your space.* A huge stack of papers here, dirty dishes there. Who can think clearly in all this chaos? Messy areas produce messy minds, and can distract you from finishing your work. To create a clutter-free zone, set up a small office in your home. And don't think you need a huge desk or a large space to set up shop. A portable computer caddy can fit in the smallest places, and you can keep your papers and office supplies neatly organized in file boxes and folders.

6. *Reward yourself.* Why wait to land a dream job in order to do something special for yourself? To stay motivated and off the couch, you've got to spoil yourself every step of the way. If you managed to mail ten resumes, take yourself out to dinner and a movie. If you've finished all your chores for the day, take an hour to watch your favorite TV show or bum around in the backyard. With so much incentive, there's really no excuse to get lazy.

gone halfway down the list, and although I'm no closer to finding my true calling, I feel that I'm moving forward and doing what makes me happy.

Trap 5. "I Don't Want to Grow UP"

When I was 14 years old, all I wanted was to turn 16. When I hit 18, I couldn't wait to celebrate 21. We spend all our lives wishing to be older and more mature only to wind up trying to turn back the clock and go back to a simpler time.

Whether you're 21 or 40, it only takes a few days at home to feel as if you're 13 again. As noble as our intentions are to maintain our adult and independent status at home, one whiff of our mother's home cooking and a snide remark from our little sis is enough to send us back into the days of our childhood. No matter how much you guard against it, expect to slip back into your wonder years just a little bit. After all, that's partly the reason you're home to begin with.

For all your posturing and grandstanding about being an adult, there's a part of you that wants to be comforted, loved unconditionally, and told that everything is going to be okay. There's a part of you that wants to be treated like a child and revert to a time when your toughest decision meant choosing between the red and yellow Legos or between Western Barbie and Beach Barbie.

Having lived through and survived our share of callous bosses, unrewarding jobs, fickle friends, hole-in-the-wall apartments, and maybe even a major life crisis or two, it's not that abnormal to crave a little peace, quiet, and relaxation. In fact, it's to be expected.

> It was my parents' decision for me to live at home while I adjusted to the real world and become more responsible and appreciative. I felt that since they were making me live at home, I might as well make the most of it. I hardly spent any money on food and did not contribute to rent. I actually got a small allowance so I could go out with my friends—talk about reverting back to being a child! It was more my father's idea to keep me home, so my mom felt bad and would spoil me now and then. I definitely became less independent and self-sufficient. Certain things I got used to doing at school, like making or buying my own food and doing my bed and laundry, were all taken care of for me.
>
> —Jeanette, 23, New York, NY

Provided your childhood was relatively trauma free, it can be very tempting to hole up in your room, read magazines all day, and pretend you're still a teenager. The sense of security can be very enticing at a time when everything seems scary and uncertain. Problem is, too much comfort and coddling can lead to laziness, apathy, and, ultimately, regression. So while you want to enjoy the comforts of home, don't get sucked in too deep unless you want to risk the possibility that you may never want to leave. Here are some tips from fellow boomerangers who successfully avoided the regression trap.

Elina's Remedy: Everyone loves to be taken care of, which is why so many of us revert to childish behavior when we come home. So why not flip the script and spoil your parents for a change? When I was living at home, I would pack my mom and sister gourmet lunches each day. By doing that, I accomplished several objectives.

It made me happy to contribute to the household and they were thrilled with the in-house catering. They loved that I was nurturing them and appreciated me even more. But best of all, I felt like a real adult.

Cassie's Remedy: A year ago, when I moved back home with my parents, my biggest fear was that I would relapse back to my childhood habits. You see, my parents are too nice for their own good. They never nag, never tell me what to do, and are usually supportive. Great, right? Don't be too sure. If you're a chronic procrastinator like me, you need all the external motivation you can get. So the first thing I did was to call a meeting with my parents. I told them how I see this living situation as a temporary arrangement and how I didn't want to be treated like a child. Finally, I asked them to compose a wish list for me with everything they wanted me to accomplish while I was home. You should have seen the list—I had to cut it in half—but it really showed that I wanted to be taken seriously.

**Act Your Age:
Eight Tips for Getting Started**

Racking up adult points is easy if you treat it like a game. Complete one challenge each week and you'll feel instantly older. Even if you don't feel grown-up, fake it for a while until it feels more natural.

1. Eliminate any childhood memorabilia from your room.
2. Act grateful and pleased when your family does something nice for you. Feelings of entitlement will make you seem like a spoiled brat.
3. Help your parents around the house even when they don't ask.
4. Don't consult with your family and friends on everything. Take time out to make some decisions on your own.
5. Avoid making excuses if you're caught doing something wrong. Admit to what you've done and give a heartfelt apology.
6. Invest in some plants and take care of them regularly. It will give you a sense of responsibility and something to do each day.
7. Treat your parent's friends and extended family as if they were your peers. You'll feel instantly older if you can slap old Uncle Bob on the back or talk politics over a family dinner.
8. Offer financial or emotional advice to your parents.

Graydon's Remedy: I think paying rent, even a small amount of $200 per month, made a big difference for me. Handing over the check every month reminded my parents that times had changed and that I was no longer the same little kid who lived with them in high school. Also, if someone's constantly paying for you they tend to want to control everything you do. Even though they still tried to pester me once in a while, they pretty much left me to my own devices. I have to think that the rent thing helped a lot. I respected myself more and I think my parents did, too.

GLASS HALF FULL: THE FIVE HIDDEN BENEFITS OF MOVING HOME

Quick: What's your favorite thing about moving back home? What will you miss most when you move out on your own again?

Before you mutter, "Nothing," and "Beats me," under your breath, take a minute to think about it. Are you absolutely sure there's nothing redeeming about being back home?

Stop me if you think this sounds maddeningly optimistic, but as I see it, there's always a silver lining to every cloud. We all know living at home has its share of drawbacks. After all, if everything was picture-perfect on the home front, you probably wouldn't be reading this book. Whether your parents are bugging you to no end, you have virtually no privacy to speak of, or your life is in a permanent state of flux, you're probably all too familiar with the pitfalls of moving back home.

Still, that doesn't mean that it's all bad. After all, there's got to be a bright side to all of this. If you're hard-pressed and too down-trodden to see the upside of things, don't worry. This section will remind you that home isn't always the worst place to be. In fact, you may even come to appreciate the experience—provided you start focusing on the positive.

1. Where the Heart Is

I can go on and on like I do with my friends, telling you I moved home to save money, get my life together, and all the million of

other sensible reasons. And it's true, those things were a major consideration. But mostly it was because I got tired of being away from my family. I thought that moving cross-country would make me more independent and strong, but all it did was make me more homesick. I missed hanging out with my parents— barbecues in the backyard, watching stupid TV shows together, talking about what we did that day. No one tells you how lonely it is to be out there on your own. Coming home to an empty apartment night after night can be the most depressing feeling in the world. Being home again has made me appreciate my parents even more.

—Denise, 24, Northampton, MA

Awww . . . here's where we get to my favorite stuff: the touchy-feely, home-sweet-home bit. In a world where everyone seems to be out for themselves and no one seems to care about little old you, being the apple of your parents' eyes can alleviate some of the pressure of the real world.

Whether it was our professors taking time to help us after class, our RA advisor coming in to save the day, or our parents sending us care baskets and helping us through the tough times, somehow we got it into our heads that this is the way life should be.

We arrived at our first job expecting people to be friendly, to take time to introduce themselves, or to at least consider our feelings before taking all the credit for our hard work. Not only that, we half-hoped that our roommates would bring us hot chicken soup when we were sick in bed. But when none of these things happened, we pouted and remembered our days at home with fondness, kicking ourselves for not taking more advantage of the good times.

It's true, many of us love our parents. We love everything about them—the way they spoil us, make us feel secure, support our every decision, and take our side in every situation. We hear all our friends talking about how they couldn't wait to move out, how important it is to be independent, how annoying it is when their parents call late at night—but all we can think about is how we can't wait to get home to call our mom or dad.

With so many boomerangers citing a need to be close to their loved ones as the reason they moved home, the conventional disciplinarian parent-child relationship of "do as I say" is slowly waning. If you ask your friends, you'd be surprised at just how many share a tight bond with their families. And no matter how much we try to deny it, sometimes we have to admit that there's nothing wrong with being good friends with our parents. In fact, at a time when nothing seems to be going right, it can be comforting to know they'll always be there.

2. Clearing Out the Skeletons

I had no choice but to move home. I was living with my mother and stepdad and was worried that all the old issues would come up. My stepdad always tried to control my life and I was always pissed at my mom for not defending me. It was kind of a sore spot in our relationship, and I never really forgave her. At first, I thought I would go insane. Absolutely nothing had changed. My stepdad was still telling me what do and my mom was on his side. I was really frustrated and angry with both of them. But I decided that I wouldn't blow up at them and yell like I used to. Even though it killed me to do it, I stayed calm and explained what was bothering me. I think the fact that I talked to them together and didn't pit them against each other helped a lot, because soon we were getting along much better. It's not perfect, but I'm beginning to understand where they're coming from.

Emily, 28, Durham, NC

If you're like the rest of the human population, you've probably got a host of unresolved issues from your childhood. Whether Mom liked your brother best or Dad was a workaholic who was never around to watch your Little League game, very few of us escaped adolescence without our fair share of emotional scars.

When all is said and done, there are only two ways of dealing with our baggage—we can either deny that we have issues or confront them head-on. We can either spend all our hard-earned cash on therapy—all the while avoiding your family's phone calls—or use time at home to try to resolve past conflicts. Of course, that's not to say that you couldn't or shouldn't do both. Many boomer-angers report using their time at home to confront their past as well as to go to therapy as a means of coping with it.

If you've found yourself smack-dab in the middle of what seems to be the battleground of your youth, baffled as to how you've managed to end up in the one place you've swore you'd never return to, why not try to use that time to deal with some of

---

Barreling Down Memory Lane

It's not often you get the chance to revisit your childhood. Believe me, when you're a little older and have a family of your own, you'll be grateful for taking time to remember the good old days. Okay, they may not all be that good. In fact, many of the memories you unearth may be painful, embarrassing—even downright traumatic at times. But whatever you find, you shouldn't try to deny any part of your past. The painful memories are just as important as the good ones, since they've all played a major part in making you who you are today. Once you have completed each mission, jot down some of your thoughts and feelings. You'll be surprised at what you find.

1. Spend the afternoon with your mother looking over old photos. Ask her what she felt, how she remembers you, and what comes to mind when she looks at the photos. Then, repeat the process with your dad. Think about how they differ in their reactions.
2. Take a weekend to sort through all your childhood memorabilia—photos, playbills, old journals. You can even make a project out of it by creating a scrapbook or memory book. Think about how you felt during each phase of your life and really explore the feelings that emerge.
3. Take a drive through some of your old haunts—the mall, high school, a favorite diner. Spend some time visiting each place to recall some of the experiences you had there.
4. Call some of your old friends and arrange to visit. Pay attention to how all of you *have* changed since your last meeting. Ask them what they thought of you way back then and how they think you've changed.
5. Reserve some time to visit your grandparents and other relatives. They also remember you when you were young and may have some memories to impart that your parents can't provide.

the unresolved conflicts of the past? Replaying your childhood traumas isn't anyone's favorite way of spending a Sunday afternoon. But isn't it better that you confront these issues now than have to face them when you're older, more set in your ways, and unwilling to change?

3. The Secret of Your Success

We all want to have a thriving social life, but think about how much of your time is spent maintaining your friends and your personal life. Just think of what you could do with all that time you spend yakking on the phone or hanging out at bars. I know one girl who squanders about four hours every day either on the phone or meeting with friends (and that doesn't even include the two hours she takes to get ready). Her social life is a full-time job in and of itself. And while that may be a good way to maintain your friendships, it doesn't leave much time for taking over the world.

While it may suck to feel like an exile with no personal life to speak of, taking a temporary break from your social life can allow you to focus on getting your career on track. If you're living in the suburbs, you may have a long commute home. Even so, not making any plans for after work once or twice a week will enable you to stay longer and put in more effort on the job. And while it may seem like a tough trade-off, it may help you get ahead professionally.

4. Never Look Back

Moving back home reminded me why I left to begin with. I stayed for a couple of months and after listening to my parents fight and criticize me and each other, I resolved to never put myself at their mercy again. Before that I always kind of coasted through life, going from job to job, always complaining and never satisfied. I guess I took my independence for granted. But moving in with my parents was a reality check that I sorely needed. Since then, I've held down the same job for two years and am working hard to support myself. I'm grateful I had that time at home because now I know how important it is for me to be on my own.

—James, 34, Ann Arbor, MI

While some boomerangers are likely to become more dependent on their parents, living at home can sometimes have the opposite effect. It can actually make you fiercely motivated to get out on your own. Having lived with roommates, we assume that life at home won't be that much different. We figure: "Hey, it'll be just like living on my own, without paying rent." And while that may be the case for some boomerangers, others don't have such easygoing relationships with their parents.

Once we get home, we're often reminded of all the reasons we left. We recall how much we hated being told what to do, how much we enjoyed having our own fridge, and a lot of other stuff we may have taken for granted. In our scurry to get home, we somehow forget all the benefits of living on our own. The old saying, "You don't know what you've got, until it's gone," never seemed more fitting. And while you may feel trapped for a little while, you can use the time to your advantage by becoming more conscious of all the issues—lack of follow-through, poor spending habits, career dissatisfaction—that brought you home in the first place.

5. Cleaning Up Our Acts

> My parents have more structure in their lives than I do. When I lived at home I wasn't eating from a can, doing dishes at 2 A.M., and running out to work ten minutes late, leaving laundry flung around the house like I'm likely to do now that it's just me living on my own. They taught me how to have more order in my life and it's helped me a lot.
>
> —Stephen, 27, Mendota, IL

No matter how much we hate all the nagging our parents do, would we really get as much done without it? As young tykes, cleaning our room or making our bed seemed like an aggravating, pointless chore. But as we got older, we adopted these habits and thanked our parents for giving us the skills to become self-sufficient and self-cleaning adults. We may even have nagged our roommates when they didn't pick up after themselves, musing at how odd it was that we sounded so much like our parents.

Now that we've returned home, there may be plenty of other

positive behaviors we can learn from our parents. Watching your mom or dad cook a nutritious meal every night may inspire you to start eating more healthily or even learn to master some recipes on your own. And seeing them go off to work every morning may inspire you to follow their lead and get a job of your own.

No matter how old we get, we still have so much to learn from our parents. After all, everyone has something to teach us. And if seeing our parents act maturely on a daily basis can make us a little more responsible, then that's a risk we have to be willing to take.

WHAT COLOR IS MY . . . WHAT?

I lived at home for so long because salaries in publishing are notoriously low. But it's not like I have so many options being an English major. I could either be a book editor, magazine editor, or freelance writer—and none of those jobs offered me the security I wanted. Finally, I decided that if I was ever going to be really financially comfortable, I would have to change fields. Problem was I really never thought about what other job would make me happy. I considered grad school, but couldn't really see myself going into even more debt. Finally, I decided that real estate might not be so bad and I went through a program and got my broker's license. Living at home gave me the chance to really figure out what kind of lifestyle I wanted and what career would get me there fastest.

—Jennifer, 28, Boca Raton, FL

So you hate your job, do you? Well, join the rest of the free world. Unlike most people who just go to their job day after day, do the requisite face time, and then collect their checks at the end of the week, today's young adults aren't satisfied with the idea of work for work's sake. And rightfully so! After all, why shouldn't we try to get a job that challenges us, stimulates us, and taps into our core talents? It's not as if we spent four years in college only to end up doing mindless work in those birdcage cubicles we've come to call home.

Financial problems, unemployment, and career transitions are cited as some of the top reasons for moving back home. It's no wonder! The jobless rate among young adults is ridiculously high. And these days, graduating college no longer means having to pick from a slew of appealing opportunities. With the pressure of paying down debt and getting a first apartment, we often find ourselves having to take the first job offered. Since we can't afford to be picky, we end up toiling away in a field we don't like or even really understand, for that matter. And after a few years of servitude, you just now may be coming out of your career fog to demand a better career, a better lifestyle, and a grander life purpose.

Not to rain on your parade, but making a career transition isn't as easy as just switching jobs. While switching jobs can often lead to greater wealth and prestige, changing careers or industries can cause salaries to plummet dramatically. Those of you hoping to make a career transition will probably have to take entry-level, low-paying jobs to make up for a lack of experience. Some even may have to complete a nonpaying internship in their late twenties in an effort to break into a competitive industry.

A transition may require that you downgrade certain areas of your life, go back to school for additional training, and relocate to your family's house for an extended period. I don't have to tell you that all these things can severely dampen your enthusiasm. But what's the alternative? Spending the rest of your life watching the clock and dreading getting up every morning? While you may have to make some concessions now, it may be worthwhile once you're happily situated in your chosen career. And if you don't make the switch while you're still relatively young, adventurous, and obligation-free, when exactly are you going to do it?

Of course, with unemployment rates still high, making a career transition may be the last thing on your mind. For some of you, just getting a job, *any* job, in this tight market is challenging enough.

Since many of you have been out in the workforce and know a thing or two about landing a gig, forgive me if I skip the "job-hunting" preliminaries. I won't bore you with resume tips or advice on writing killer cover letters. But don't despair. I've included a brief primer on breaking into a tough market that both recent college grads and seasoned pros will benefit from. This chapter will also address early to midcareer boomerangers as they try to brainstorm new career objectives or discover their inner entrepreneur, as well as draw up a concrete game plan for breaking into their chosen field. For those of you considering going back to school to further your careers, you'll find out how to evaluate the pros and cons of graduate school, as well as advice for choosing a practical program that will pay off in the long run. So if you're tired of putting your career on automatic pilot, want to get proactive, and are ready to do something you love for a change, you've come to the right place.

THE IN-BETWEEN: MAKING A CAREER TRANSITION

If the prospect of a root canal has become more appealing than a day at the office, you may be in dire need of a career change. But first ask yourself: Are you sick of your job specifically or the entire career? When it comes to career transitions, it's very easy to mistake the trees for the forest. So make sure you're really ready for a complete overhaul before deciding to switch.

If you've returned home for the sole purpose of finding your life's passion, true calling, or whatever you want to call it, take heart; you're not alone. There are millions of young adults in the same shoes, dying to make a clean break. There are many ways to discover what floats your boat professionally, but the one thing you can't do is approach the matter willy-nilly. That's how you ended up working in a field you hate in the first place. If you're really going to give this career thing a fair shot and use your time at home to find your ideal vocation, you'll need to approach the matter methodically. That's why I've included a step-by-step plan for the boomeranger in transition. But before you start, ask yourself: What is it I'm really after?

- More job security?
- Better pay?
- Nicer location?
- More opportunity to travel?
- Improved teamwork?
- Greater challenges?
- More flexibility and time off?

Step 1. Analyze

With so many industries and careers to choose from, you'll probably feel overwhelmed trying to decide which one is right for you. That's why it's so important to figure out your strengths, weaknesses, and preferences before evaluating your prospects. You should jot down your answers on a separate sheet of paper so you can review your responses later.

Likes: It's really simple. Here's where you jot down all the things you enjoy doing—favorite hobbies, TV shows, job tasks. And don't self-censor. Even if you enjoy playing video games all day, that's a legitimate hobby that many people have turned into careers. So list everything you can think of—and don't hold back!

My likes are:

1. _____

2. _____

3. _____

4. _____

5. _____

6. _____

7. _____

8. _____

9. _____

10. _____

Vision: Once you get a handle on what you like, think about your vision for life. What is it that you really want to contribute? While some people want to make the world a better place, others want to start a business or work for a start-up where there's lots of energy and excitement. It's important that you figure this out, since getting

a job that's in alignment with that vision will make you more successful in the long run.

My vision is:

1. _____
2. _____
3. _____
4. _____
5. _____
6. _____
7. _____
8. _____
9. _____
10. _____

Must-haves: Here is where you figure out all the requirements that need to be met in your next job. Must-haves include items like location, title, salary, company size, and benefits. Once you figure out what you absolutely can't do without, write it down for handy reference.

My must-haves are:

1. _____
2. _____
3. _____
4. _____
5. _____
6. _____

7. _____

8. _____

9. _____

10. _____

Talents: As evidenced by David Letterman's "Stupid Human Tricks" segment, everyone has a talent. Oh come on, stop being so modest! You don't have to break a world record to qualify something as a talent. Think back to your past jobs, volunteer activities, and academic history for inspiration. Whether you're good at writing, speaking, negotiating, mediating, or typing, make sure to specify each and every talent in the blanks below.

My talents are:

1. _____

2. _____

3. _____

4. _____

5. _____

6. _____

7. _____

8. _____

9. _____

10. _____

Quirks: Matching your personality to your future career is crucial to your success. If you're painfully shy, you probably shouldn't go into a highly extroverted career like public relations or sales. Or, if you're a highly creative, restless type, it might not make sense to get a job in a rigid, nine-to-five desk job. Whatever career you pick,

it's important that you feel comfortable in that setting. Here's your chance to describe your personality—quirks, complexes, insecurities, and all.

My quirks are:

1. _____

2. _____

3. _____

4. _____

5. _____

6. _____

7. _____

8. _____

9. _____

10. _____

Step 2. Investigate

Now that you've taken a good long look at yourself and have a better understanding of your likes, temperament, and talents, it's time to investigate your job prospects. According to Justine Reichman, founder of the Career Change Network (www.careerchangenet work.com), most people in career transition have unrealistic ideas about their target industries. That's why it's so important to do your research. The last thing you want to do is invest any more time or money training yourself for a career you're ill-suited for or one that won't live up to the hype.

Browse Online. There are plenty of comprehensive resources to help you get the 411 on your target industry. These days, you can get industry statistics, growth projections, and descriptions of almost any occupation under the sun. Here are some online resources that should give you a better idea of what you'll be getting into:

- ➐ Vault Industry List (www.vault.com/hubs/industrylist.jsp)   This site is a gold mine of career information. You can check out stats and educational requirements for many fields, including finance, marketing, new media, health, and nonprofit. You'll also find articles and the latest news about each industry. And if you really want to know what it feels like to work at each company, sign up for a premium membership to browse the "Workplace Surveys" feature.

- ➐ WetFeet (www.wetfeet.com)   This comprehensive website is your one-stop shop for industry- and career-related information. You can check out specific interviewing advice, extensive career and industry profiles, and real-people interviews so you can get a better sense of the on-the-job, day-to-day experience.

- ➐ Monster.com Job Profiles (www.jobprofiles.monster.com/)   You won't find a shortage of job options at this neatly organized site. With careers running the gamut from A to Z—including tattoo designer and FBI agent—each profile includes education and skill requirements, and long-term industry projections.

- ➐ Occupational Outlook Handbook (www.bls.gov/oco)   If you want the official guide to careers, look no further than this definitive source for career research compiled annually by the U.S. Department of Labor Statistics. You'll find all the updated industry stats, job descriptions, education and accreditation requirements, as well as salary potential.

Hot Jobs   Wouldn't it be great to look into a crystal ball to find out which professions will be most in demand? Well, now you can. While it's always a good idea to figure out what you're good at *before* picking a new career, you should also find out which industries are set to grow—especially if you've rated job security and growth potential high on your big-picture goals list. According to the U.S. Department of Labor, these are some of the sectors that will be enjoying steady or explosive growth from the years 2002–2012.

Health Services: Longer life expectancy and a huge aging population contribute to a projected growth rate of 31.8 percent. That's faster than any other industry. In fact, about one out of four new jobs created in the United States will be in health care and social assistance, including residential care facilities, private hospitals, and nursing. If you've ever considered a career in health care, now is definitely time to think about getting additional training.

Professional/Business Services: With the increase of new technology and the growing complexity of business, this group, which includes administrative support, scientific services, and technical support, will increase 30.4 percent, adding five million new jobs in the coming years.

Information Services: If you're thinking of going into or are already in any of the information-related services (publishing, broadcasting, Internet database, cable industry, telecommunications, Internet search engines, wireless services, Internet publishing, or Internet service providers), you're in luck! Employment in these industries is expected to grow by an average of 52 percent from 2002 to 2012.

Hospitality Industry: The Department of Labor is confident that with higher incomes (let's take their word for it), dual-income families, and more leisure time, employment in hotels, the arts, restaurants, amusement facilities, and gaming facilities is set to increase by a whopping 17.8 percent.

According to the U.S. Department of Labor and the book *Best Jobs for the 21st Century* (Third Edition, JIST Works), these are some of the fastest-growing occupations:

Nurses	Personal home care aides
Computer software engineers	Sales managers
Postsecondary teachers	Physical therapists
Network computer administrators	Truck drivers
Retail salespeople	Database administrators
Desktop publishers	Veterinary technologists and
Customer service representatives	technicians
Social service assistants	Receptionists
General and operational	
managers	

Go to the Source. Hopefully by now you've narrowed down your options and have a better idea of what you want to do. Now you'll need to set up informational interviews with professionals in the field. While browsing interviews and occupation profiles are all well and good, there's something to say for getting it straight from the horse's mouth. You may be able to extract more relevant and detailed information, as well as find leads for future opportunities. Your best bet for finding people to interview is to ask friends, neighbors, and relatives for any and all leads. You can also check out the alumni network at your university, where former classmates sign up in order to assist people just like you in finding fulfilling and meaningful vocations. Once you have set up your meetings, make sure to bring a list of questions along. And don't even think about hitting up your chosen expert for a job. The interviews are for informational purposes only. If they choose to recommend you for a position or know of a suitable job opportunity, it's their role to take the lead.

Visit a Career Counselor/Job Coach. If you have a few extra dollars to plunk down, hiring a career counselor or job coach may be the best money you ever spend. Think of it as an investment in your future. Your career counselor will set up a one-on-one meeting, administer several personality and job aptitude tests, and will listen carefully as you discuss your life goals, dreams, and ambitions. She/he will then find patterns and themes that reveal what you are best suited for and how you can reach your goals. Career coaches can also help you deal with common problems like time management, disorganization, and motivation. Not only can they point you in the right direction, many of them will also schedule follow-up visits so you can stay on track as you search for your ideal job. To find a counselor in your area, contact the Career Counselors Consortium at 212-859-3515 or visit www.career.org.

Step 3. Work It!

Now that you've analyzed and investigated, it's time to take action. It's easy to get boggled by all the possibilities, so make sure you start doing something to pursue your goals right away. As soon as you feel you have a good idea of what you want to do, don't waste time launching your new job hunt. After all, the sooner you make your career transition, the sooner you can get out on your own again.

Transfer Your Skills. Remember how tough it was to transfer to a new school or enter college as a freshman? Starting from scratch in a new industry can be a daunting proposition, especially if you had a certain amount of seniority in your old position. But what many people don't realize is that you don't have to start from ground zero in making a career transition. The key is to find out which of your skills and abilities are transferable to your new industry. For example, if you're looking to switch from public relations to advertising, you may want to emphasize your project and client-management skills, since both fields place a high premium on these abilities. So if you're reticent about starting as an intern in your mid-twenties, here are some strategies for avoiding entry-level hell.

> Check out job descriptions that you're interested in to determine which skills you'll need. Then create a master list of desirable skills for each field you're considering.

> Make a list of every job, internship, and volunteer activity you've worked at. Analyze which skills you used or improved upon at each job. Here are some skills you may have acquired: communicating, organizing, supervising, planning, negotiating, delegating, troubleshooting, researching.

Job: _____

Skill 1: _____

Skill 2: _____

Skill 3: _____

Job: _____

Skill 1: _____

Skill 2: _____

Skill 3: _____

Job: _____

Skill 1: _____

Skill 2: _____

Skill 3: _____

Job: _____

Skill 1: _____

Skill 2: _____

Skill 3: _____

➐ Draft a cover letter and skills-based resume that shows each prospective employer how you plan to apply your skills to their position.

Break the Rules. You can follow all the rules and never get to where you want to be. That's why you'll need to think on your feet and take some risks, especially since you really don't have time to waste. If you've tried all the run-of-the-mill job search strategies and have had no luck, expedite your job search with these surefire tips.

➐ *Focus on the Bottom Line.* Show the company how you will be able to contribute and add value by writing a cover letter that shows you're the person for the job. Sending a list of prior jobs or resume with just your work history won't inspire anyone to hire you.

➐ *Show No Fear.* Just as with dating, acting desperate to get a job can cost you big-time! If you're sending a letter, avoid phrases like, "I'm looking for a position," or "Please consider me." Write a letter stating that you're looking to upgrade your job and describe how you see yourself fitting into the company. Employers can smell desperation a mile away, so remember to act confident.

➐ *Fuhgetaboutit.* Hunting for a job is a grueling process. To avoid burnout, you'll need to take a mental break every once in a while. Think of it as your time to recharge, revive, and recover. Whether you take a day or a week off, avoid thinking about the job hunt and do something you love.

➐ *Ask Why!* If you're rejected for a job, don't forget to ask what disqualified you from the position. While it may make you and the HR person feel uncomfortable, you will probably get some pointers as to what you can do to make yourself more appealing in the future. Trust me, you can't buy this kind of feedback.

➐ *Create a Job.* Why wait for a company to open a position when you can create one with a little bit of ingenuity and research? If there's a company you're dying to work for but they have no openings, do some investigating to find out which departments need your help. Once you figure out how you can contribute, contact a manager and explain the position to be created and what you can bring to the enterprise. As farfetched as this idea may seem, it's worked for some people and it might just work for you.

THE UNEMPLOYED: COPING WITH JOB LOSS

I remember being so angry when I first got laid off from my job as an account sales executive. I had given so much to the company and when they let me go, it felt like being betrayed by my best friend. Not only that, finding out that my boss had been bad-mouthing me the whole time to the senior staff was extremely painful. I had all these feelings and I just bottled them up. I tried to look for a new job while living at home, but my heart really wasn't in it. I finally gave myself a few months just to recover and do nothing just so I could get over what happened.

—Stan, 34, Portland, OR

The statistics are staggering. According to the Bureau of Labor Statistics, the number of unemployed 20- to 24-year-olds jumped from 6.7 percent in September 2000 to 9.3 percent as of July 2004. For 25- to 34 year-olds, the number of those unemployed rose from 3.7 percent to 6.3 percent. Whether you were laid off, downsized, scaled back, or quit in a blaze of glory, being unemployed can take a toll on you. At first it may seem that you'll never get enough of

ELINAFURMAN

sleeping in, staying out late, and catching up on your to-dos (wash hair, buy beer, read horoscope), but eventually you may actually want to go back to work. Not only that, with your parents bugging you every five minutes about finding a job, you may find that your self-esteem and confidence had plummeted to an all-time low. Of course, the prospect of looking for a job can be trying to say the least. Dealing with rejection, unanswered phone calls, and slamming doors isn't anyone's idea of a good time. So if you're having difficulty coping with your newfound unemployed status, following these strategies may help you regain your footing.

Pick a Job, Any Job

Some boomerangers think that unemployment is the same as landing the "get-out-of-job-free" card. But unless you're writing the great American novel, starting a business, or regrouping after a painful ordeal, there's really no excuse for not working. Just because you're looking for your ideal position doesn't mean you can't take a part-time, survival job to tide you over. If you've been hunting for work for more than six months and you still can't find anything, you may want to consider a temporary gig. Even if it's a retail or food services position, bringing in money every month will keep you from feeling ineffectual and will allow you to contribute to the household expenses. Another benefit is that by maintaining a consistent work record, you'll avoid gaps on your resume that some companies may find unacceptable. And besides, in some states you can earn as much as a third of your unemployment insurance benefits before the state deducts money from your weekly check. See? Now you have no excuse.

Be Good to Yourself

Staying mentally and physically spry during your employment hiatus may keep you from sliding into a deep funk. Keep your brain and skills sharp by reading industry mags and books you've been meaning to get to. You should also take advantage of your time off by getting into better shape. Take walks around the block, join an inexpensive gym, or invest in a workout video that you can do in the privacy of your own room. Not only will you feel and look better, you'll have more energy for the job hunt. Being good to yourself also means surrounding yourself with warm and caring people. If you find that your parents and friends are becoming more critical about your unemployed status, reach out and ask them for their support and consideration. You may just be surprised when they deliver.

Get Some Structure

Since most of us plan our days around our jobs, not having one can put a serious crimp in our efforts to stay disciplined and organized. With no markers in place and nowhere to be, it's very easy to lose track of time during your day. The last thing you want to do is to dramatically change your habits during this transitional time. Once you're out of a job, try to keep your schedule as it was while you were working. Impose a routine on yourself by setting times for waking up, working, eating, sleeping, and socializing.

What's So Funny?

It's a proven fact that people who can see the humor in a situation, however dire, tend to be healthier, happier, and more successful. And while dealing with rejection, dim-witted HR personnel, and other job-search shenanigans can be hard, it can also be pretty damn funny. If you're having a hard time seeing the humor in your particular situation, check out these sites, which are bound to give you something to smile about.

➐ www.oddtodd.com Todd Rosenberg, otherwise known as "Odd Todd," has been laid off and he's not going to take it anymore. Chronicling his post-layoff life of long naps and potato chip dinners, Odd Todd's flash-animated cartoons and games will keep you in stitches. If you're feeling especially generous, you can leave a dollar or more in the virtual tip jar.

- www.unemployedtheo.com   Unemployed Theo (aka U.T.) reenacts his life as a laid-off, couch-loafing dude in easily digestible and funny movie shorts.

- www.askyourass.com   Michael Laskoff, the author of *Landing on the Right Side of Your Ass: A Survival Guide for the Recently Unemployed,* offers practical advice and tips with a side of wry sense of humor.

THE GRADUATE: EVALUATING GRAD SCHOOL

The reason I started thinking about attending law school is because as a paralegal, I was often forced to do the same amount of work for a lot less money. I figured going to law school would at least guarantee me some real money down the line. And I already had so much work experience in the area. Problem was, the more I considered law school, the less certain I became. Not only did I not particularly like the work involved, I didn't really see myself going to school for four more years. I finally decided to get my master's in education. It would only take two years and give me the chance to work with kids, which I love.

—Sally, 27, Madison, WI

With so many boomerangers returning home to pursue an advanced degree, it would seem that attending grad school would be a no-brainer. Living at home and going to school gives you a solid excuse for shacking up with the parentals, since people won't be as likely to wonder what's wrong with you if you tell them that you're studying to become a doctor or getting your Ph.D. in nuclear physics. And it can make you richer beyond your wildest dreams, right? Shell out thousands of dollars now for double or even triple that in income later. Seems like a simple enough proposition to grasp. But can it really be this clear-cut? If it was, then tens of thousands of boomerangers wouldn't be so conflicted about the prospect of going back. There's the time commitment, all those books and paper to write, and a lot more debt to pay off. And what if you don't find a job after school? While most grad students end up working in their field, many are forced to chalk up their considerable graduate school loan as a loss due to a lack of interest or op-

BOOMERANGNATION

portunities in their field. To go to school or not to go? That really is the question. Here's a quick primer to help you make the decision:

The Pros

Real Genius: A mind is a terrible thing to waste. Even if your degree isn't the most practical (see master's of fine arts, philosophy, nineteenth-century American literature), you can still claim to be a more educated, intellectually stimulated, and well-rounded person than most. That has to count for something, right?

More Opportunity: An advanced degree can, in some cases, significantly increase your job prospects and earning potential. According to the Employment Policy Foundation, people with a master's degree make $139,000 more than those with only a bachelor's degree, and professional and doctoral grads earn about $595,477 more. Of course, when you break it down annually, deduct taxes, and subtract school loans, the difference doesn't seem as mind-blowing.

Credibility: Whether you're planning to publish, work as a consultant, or become a small business owner, having a master's degree or doctorate can significantly increase how seriously people take you. You'd be surprised just how quickly people defer to you in all matters of importance when they discover that you have an advanced degree. Here's another way to look at it: All things being equal, if it's between you and another candidate, your degree can give you a leg up over the competition. So if you play your cards right and know how to work it, a higher degree can be a major asset in whatever you choose to do.

The Cons

Use it or Lose It: If you get a degree and don't use it, employers will either think you're overqualified or an underachiever. Make sure you're legitimately interested in the field or that the skills you acquire in the program can be easily transferred to other industries.

In Debt for Life. Unless your parents have offered to spring for the whole thing, you'll have to borrow. If you're attending a top program for two years or more, it's not uncommon to have school loans totaling over $100,000. Ask yourself: Can you honestly live with this number?

Lost Income: Taking out more loans may be bad enough, but it's not the full extent of your financial commitment. If you're planning to attend school full-time, you'll need to consider how much money you would have been making had you worked during those years. So if you were bringing home about $40,000 per year and signed up for a two-year program, that's eighty thousand big ones that you could have pocketed.

Does Not Apply: If your target field is extremely obscure or specialized (think ancient Mesoamerican writing) you may have a hard time applying your research to a real world setting. Sure, you can become the world's foremost expert on the topic, but if there isn't a great enough demand for the information, you may find that your window of opportunity narrows considerably.

TOP FIVE QUESTIONS ABOUT GRAD SCHOOL

Only five? While you may have a gazillion questions about graduate school, you may want to start by checking out the five most common ones. Of course, this doesn't mean you should stop here. One of the most important steps in evaluating whether grad school is right for you will be to talk to deans and admissions counselors at a few schools. They can provide specific advice about your field of study and answer questions that have to do with your particular circumstances. In the meanwhile, let's get started.

Question 1. Am I Postponing the Inevitable?

If you're going to law school or business school just because you don't know what to do with your life, don't be so hasty. Graduate school should not be used to escape, avoid, or defer living in the real world. Nor is it a good place to hide out to avoid a weak economy. So if that's why you're going, stop right there! You may not be the ideal candidate. Another poor excuse for going to school is sentimentality. Many boomerangers get tired of the daily grind and think back fondly to their wild college days. But can you really go back? The answer, of course, is no. The graduate and undergraduate experience couldn't be more different. So if a desire to relive the good old days and get out of your current job is all that's motivating you, you may want to take more time to consider your options.

Question 2. What Should I Study?

Here's the thing about graduate school: It's not the best place to explore your options. To make it in grad school, you'll need to be determined, focused, and 100 percent sure that you want to pursue your course of study. So if you're still undecided or hemming and hawing about what field to enter, you may need more time to think it over. Once you enter school, you'll need to be ultracommitted and really love what you're doing in order to keep up with the rigors of the program. One way to gauge your level of interest is to take a course or two before enrolling. That way you can measure your tolerance for the subject matter before signing on the dotted line.

Question 3. Is it Absolutely Necessary?

Unless you're looking to become a doctor, lawyer, psychologist, or a member of any other field that requires an advanced degree, consider going to grad school as a last resort. If you don't have to go and can still be successful in your chosen field, you may want to reconsider. Contrary to some opinions, graduates with an advanced degree won't be bombarded with job offers as soon as they finish school. It's important that you talk to alumni, professors, and school admission advisors before you go to find out about job prospects. If you're lucky you may even be able to score some interviews with an HR person in your chosen industry. You should ask him/her if a graduate degree will help your chances and increase your opportunities for advancement. And if the answer is yes, ask what kind (professional, doctorate, associate's degree) will get you there fastest. Once you have a better idea of what you can expect, you can figure out whether all that money is worth the extra letters after your name.

Question 4. Can I Afford It?

According to the National Association of Student Financial Aid Administrators (NASFAA), the average graduate student pursuing a master's will amass a debt load of $28,809. Now compare that number with $123,898 for dental programs, $99,225 for medical programs, and $63,078 for law school and you'll see why this is one of the most frequently asked questions.

When you're thinking of whether you can afford going to school, don't just think about the financing. Even if you do get loans, going to school can be an extremely taxing proposition. Not only are you missing work to pursue your degree, you'll also have to consider your future job prospects, time commitment, and all that you would be giving up when you enroll in a full-time program. Sometimes it's not even worth going to school, unless you can get into a top-tier institution. Take MBAs, for example. While these programs may instill you with leadership skills and help you figure out the ins and outs of financial models, you may have a hard time finding a job that justifies the exorbitant expense unless you go to a top ten school like Harvard, MIT Sloan School of Management, or the University of Chicago.

Question 5. Should I Go Full-Time or Part-Time?

If you're considering going to school part-time, you should be aware of the challenges of having to balance a full class load and an outside job. The stress of juggling this schedule can be daunting to say the least. Not only that, going to school part-time may disqualify you for fellowships, grants, and other forms of financial aid. In most programs, one has to be a full-time student in order to apply for financial assistance. Of course, if your employer is willing to pick up the tab, you should seriously consider your company's offer. Another issue that may factor into your decision is that as a part-time student you may not get the same level of service as full-timers. Certain courses may not be offered nights or weekends. You may also not have the same access to libraries, career service centers, and other facilities on campus. If you're considering moving home with your parents, don't have any dependents, and can safely afford to sacrifice your income, attending graduate school full-time may be your best course of action.

THE ENTREPRENEUR: STARTING A SMALL BUSINESS

I used to have a good job selling advertising for a prestigious local magazine but I didn't feel I had any creative outlet with them. I felt underappreciated and underutilized. On the surface I was doing a lot of fun things and seemed happy enough, but eventually I just kind of broke down. I was talking to my parents and started crying talking about how miserable I was. I hadn't even realized I was that unfulfilled and unhappy until that moment. So I started a dating company because I think there aren't a lot of good ways for singles to meet and get to know each other. I don't find that living at home has created any special challenges to starting my business. I think potentially one challenge is that it's easier to slack off because I have my DVD collection handy, but I'm usually pretty good in the self-control department. I do my website work and send out e-mails from a station in my mom's office, and most of the paperwork and planning goes on in my bedroom.

—Eric, 30, Washington, D.C.

Living the Great American Dream isn't just about owning a home. In fact, for millions of young people, it means starting and running their own business. Having come of age in a weak economy, young people want to start their own business to battle the insecurity they feel in the workplace. According to a 2000 survey conducted by *Newsweek*, Generations X and Y exhibit an unprecedented entrepreneurial spirit, with more than 65 percent of 14- to 19-year-olds being very interested in starting a business compared with about half of the general population. After years of toiling away for ungrateful management and commuting long hours, many of us can't wait to launch our enterprises.

If the nine-to-five grind is simply not for you, you may want to consider moving home in order to launch your own business. Once you factor in the costs and realize how expensive starting your own business can be, living with your parents in exchange may seem like a small price to pay. You'll be able to save a considerable amount as your company goes through its lean months of operation. So whether you're interested in starting your own online dating service, bar/restaurant, a Subway franchise, or a concierge service you can run out of your home, you couldn't have picked a better time or place to do it.

The Pros

A Gazillion Dollars: You may not become a millionaire overnight, but entrepreneurs do cite the prospect of making more moola as a draw when going out on their own. True, it often takes years to get out of the red. But some companies, especially those with low overhead, do report a profit in their first year.

Free to Be Me: Freedom and flexibility are one of the top reasons for starting your own venture. Many a young entrepreneur simply can't stomach the notion of bureaucracy, face time, and office politics. And who could blame them? If the idea of answering only to yourself, setting your own schedule, and working out of your own office appeals to your inner maverick, starting a small business may be your ticket out of corporate hell.

Only the Good Start Young: Here's the thing: If you fail now while you're still young, you can chalk it up to a learning experience and move on. If you fail when you're 50, you may become overwhelmed and have a more difficult time bouncing back. Our twenties and thirties are a time to explore, fail big, and succeed. If you don't take this chance to pursue your dreams now, when will you?

Entrepreneur Quiz: Do You Have What It Takes?

Not all of us are born entrepreneurs. In fact, unless you have initiative, passion, and plenty of moxie (or at least a business partner with all of the above), you can kiss your start-up plans good-bye. With about 75 percent of all small businesses folding in their first year, you better be sure you have what it takes to make your business a success. Take this quiz to find out if your E.Q. (Entrepreneur Quotient) is up to par.

1. You have a proposal to present to your boss next week. You:
A. Write down your plan and get started right away.
B. Think about starting in a few days.
C. Wait until the last minute and then spend the whole night worrying about the presentation.

2. That cute, single somebody you met last week invites you along on a sailing trip. You've never been sailing before, so you:
A. Jump at the chance. You've been dying to try something like this for a while.
B. Accept the invitation, but vow to bring some extra Dramamine along.
C. Decline the offer. After all, you don't want to get seasick on your first date.

3. You have a great idea for a movie script. You:
A. Buy some screenwriting software and get to work.
B. Jot down some notes and ask friends if they like the idea.
C. Put it out of your mind. It's practically impossible to sell a screenplay!

4. You're asked to head up the tenant association in your apartment building. After thinking about it, you:
A. Take the job. You're just the person to make some changes.
B. Agree to attend all the meetings, but you're not about to take all the responsibilities.
C. Refuse to get involved. Your schedule is already too crammed as is.

5. Your friend wants to set you up on a blind date. You:
A. Call the date, arrange for a time and place to meet, and hope for the best.
B. Find out everything you can about the person so you have plenty to talk about if he/she is a big bore.
C. Bow out gracefully. Blind dates are such a waste of time.

ELINAFURMAN

6. **You've been unemployed for months, when Mom calls to say she has a job lead. You:**

A. Follow up with her contact right away and arrange a meeting.

B. Call a week later to ask about the position.

C. Lose the phone number and blow it off when your mom asks about it a few months later. Who could she know?

7. **You're really pumped about the upcoming election, and want to do everything to help your favorite candidate get in office. You:**

A. Sign up as a volunteer on his/her campaign.

B. Donate a few dollars online.

C. Cross your fingers and hope for the best.

SCORING

Five or more As: Born to Launch

You're a natural-born leader and have entrepreneur potential written all over you. Not one to be content to sit on the sidelines, you give 150 percent to everything you do. Your personality and initiative should give you a head start in any endeavor your choose. Knock 'em dead!

Five or more Bs: Up and Comer

When it comes to doing something you're passionate about, there's no holding you back. But don't forget, passion is only a small piece of the entrepreneurial puzzle. As a business owner you'll need to take care of details that are often tedious and boring. That's where patience, consistency, and determination come into play. Once you develop these qualities, there'll be no stopping you.

Five or more Cs: Work in Progress

When you're starting a business there's simply no room for procrastination, indecision, or laziness. Too many things can and often do go wrong on a daily basis. Of course, just because you may not be ready to start your business now doesn't mean you can't get your act together. Start by taking on more challenges in your daily work and home life. It's all about becoming more responsible and proactive. And don't forget: Entrepreneurs aren't born, they're made.

The Cons

Living with Uncertainty: If you thought that the instability of the job market was hard to take, just try living without a steady paycheck for a year or two. While it may be liberating to cast all doubts aside and risk everything for your dream, you'll need nerves of steel to weather the precarious start-up phase. Of course, living at home with your parents is a great way to offset the financial instability.

24-7: All entrepreneurs will tell you that they eat, sleep, and breathe their work. While not having a set schedule may seem like a blessing, it can also prevent you from setting boundaries between work and personal life. When you go to work full-time, at least your weekends and nights are your own. So don't be deceived: When it comes to launching a new business, you may end up working longer and harder than you ever imagined.

THE FINAL WORD

We've all heard the expression, "Do what you love, and the money will follow." But for many of us finding our passion is easier said than done. I don't have to tell you that this is the time in your life when you're supposed to be exploring and thinking about what will truly make you happy. The key is not to worry about what others have accomplished or feel you have to do what others expect of you. Whether you're between jobs, considering going back to school, or trying to start your own business, remember that your work doesn't define who you are. Take it easy on yourself and don't feel pressured to come up with quick answers and easy solutions. While it may be uncomfortable to live in limbo while many of your peers seem to have it all together, you'll have to be able to live with a certain amount of uncertainty while you plot your new direction. After all, there will be many other times in your life when answers seem in short supply; times that will make this stage in your life seem easy in comparison. But by learning how to cope and staying flexible in times of change, you'll discover that the only formula for true and lasting success is taking life as it comes.

KA-CHING!
MINDING YOUR MONEY

You know what, I feel really good about living at home. I am meeting all of my financial goals of saving for my own place. I've even paid off my car in the process. I think it was a very mature decision to move back home, and I feel more motivated than ever because I am doing something about achieving my goals in life, rather than simply talking about it. When my friends find out about how much I'm saving in living and commuting expenses each month, they're really impressed. Several of them have even commented that they wished they had the same opportunity. Now that I'm home and taking responsibility for my finances, I feel that I have become more grounded and responsible. With housing costs so high in California, and rents being as much as mortgage payments, most people think it's a smart move. And I couldn't agree more!

—Carlos, 30, Los Angeles, CA

Picture this: It's Friday night and you're sprawled out in your old bedroom listening to your new *Garden State* CD. Your best friend in the city is having party and invites you to crash for the night. Problem is, you don't have a car. You're stuck at home for another weekend. But after yet another week working like a dog at your full-time gig, you feel entitled to a little time off. In fact, with all the money you've saved so far on rent and food, you're thinking about treating yourself. So you:

A. Book a once-in-a-lifetime cruise around the Mediterranean.
B. Drop everything, call a $50 car service to take you into the city, and blow a week's paycheck on boozing with your friends.

C. Rent a movie, make some popcorn, and think about all the money you're saving.

Most of us move home with the best of intentions. We figure, why throw away our money on rent when we can save up for major life goals, like house purchases, graduate school, or even a small business? But when it comes down to actually putting our money where our mouths are, we often find ourselves falling short of our goals.

There are dozens of stories of boomerangers who moved home to save money only to end up spending even more. Since many of us are living rent-free and have more discretionary income than we're used to, it's not unusual to indulge in a few splurge fests. After all, we work hard and we deserve to have a little fun, right? Not only that, the feeling that we're somehow missing out on our best years by living at home can often lead to what I call "therapeutic spending." Feeling trapped by our circumstances, we try to distract ourselves by spending on luxury goods, trips, nights on the town, and new outfits to make ourselves feel better. It's no wonder that we've become a prime target for market researchers hoping to separate us from our hard-earned money. With most of our daily living costs already covered, all this disposable income makes us a prime marketing demographic.

Of course, some of you don't have that luxury of saving. Many of you are just hoping to get out of the red and repair what's left of your soiled credit rating. If you're laboring under a mountain of debt, believe me, you're not alone. This is one of the most frequently cited reasons for moving back home.

When it comes to becoming financially responsible, figuring out what's most important to you is the first step. That way, when you spot an item you absolutely can't live without—new laptop, video game, iPod—you'll have a good reason for why you can. Many of us don't set goals for fear that we won't meet them. But hoping that your future takes care of itself is not enough, especially since you've already returned to ground zero by moving back home. Once you make the decision to return to the nest, it's important to make good use of your time there. After all, isn't this relatively financially stress-free period the best time to deal with your money issues?

And even if you don't have a financial goal or are trying to figure out the best strategy for your financial future, you needn't feel left out in the cold. There are plenty of ways you can put your money to good use. The four big-picture goals covered in this chapter may just inspire you to take control of your financial future once and for all!

Goal 1. Reducing Debt
Goal 2. Saving Money
Goal 3. Growing Money
Goal 4. Protecting Your Assets

THE ART OF SETTING GOALS

Do you have a goal? Well, do you? If you don't, it's high time you came up with one. After all, not only will setting goals help you move out faster and get back on your feet, it will give you something to work toward while you pass the time at home. When it comes to setting financial goals, you need to be crystal clear about what you hope to accomplish. And don't feel as if you have to do what everyone else is doing, either. Just because your best friend brags about his stock portfolio doesn't mean that your interests lie in the market. And just because your dad wants you to save for retirement doesn't mean you need to invest all your money in an IRA.

The key to becoming financially proactive is to set goals that work for *you*. If you've got wanderlust in your veins, then maybe saving for vacations makes more sense. If you're a budding musician and want to make it big in the industry, you may want to save for some recording equipment. Remember, there's no such thing as a wrong or right goal. Of course, retirement and debt are important matters that need to be addressed. But who says you can't set more than one goal? If you plan properly, you can set as many objectives as you want and meet all of them by adhering to a sound savings strategy. Here is a breakdown of three types of goals:

Immediate Goals: This is a short-term goal that you'll be able to meet in a week, a month, or a few months. You don't want to set short-term goals for longer than a year. Good examples of "immediate goals" are buying a new MP3 player, paying Mom and Dad rent, or saving for a white-water rafting trip in Costa Rica. It's important to make sure that your short-term goals are realistic. If you set your goals too high, you may not be able to keep up with the plan. If saving $100 a month for your vacation seems like too much of a strain, why not put away $50 a month instead?

Middle-of-the-Road Goals: You'll want to accomplish these goals any time between one and five years. These could include anything from paying school loans, saving a six-months' nest egg, buying a car, or paying off credit card debt.

Long-term Goals: "Where do you think you'll be in five years?" is probably right up there on the list of annoying questions. Like me, most of you probably have trouble planning a month in advance, let alone five to ten years. But if you're really going to get the most out of this boomeranging experience, you may want to at least start thinking about it. Are you planning to have a family? Buy a house? Start a business? Save for retirement? While all of these things seem like they're a million years away, eventually all or some of them will happen. Based on the kind of person you are, make some educated guesses and write them down. Once you've done that, remember to stay flexible. New goals and expenses will pop up every day. You'll want to make sure your goals evolve with the times and your circumstances. For instance, if you find that you've just come up with a brilliant invention, don't be afraid to change the game plan and put some of your savings toward your small business.

GOAL 1. REDUCING DEBT

When it comes to debt, there are no absolutes. As children, we were taught that all debt was inherently evil. We tended to see the world in black and white. Debt = Bad. Saving = Good. Hopefully by now you've learned that as with everything, debt defies such handy definitions. No matter how scary it seems to be in the red, there's very little chance that any of us will ever end up homeless, living in a box, and muttering gibberish to ourselves. But stuffing our money under the mattress won't lead to a life of ease and luxury, either. If you don't invest your savings, you'll end up losing money in the long run.

Debt isn't the monster many of us have made it out to be. In fact, there is such a thing as good debt. Anything that will appreciate in value should be seen as an investment or what we'll call "good debt." Your education, for one, is a good debt. It's an investment in your future. Real estate and business debt are also good, since the interest rate on your loan will be relatively low and the value of the investment will increase with the years.

While you may not be able to spot bad debt when you see it, most of us have plenty of it. Anything you buy that has no appreciation value (cars, boats, electronics, expensive dinners, vacations to the Caribbean) and that you'll have to finance on your credit card is a bad debt. When you buy a car or that new camcorder you've been eyeing, the value drops about 50 percent when you walk out of the store because they're items that depreciate in value. So if you paid for them on your credit card, that's bad debt, since you're going to end up paying double the original cost in interest rates. And while no one is saying that you shouldn't enjoy some goodies every now and then, putting items that have depreciating value on your credit card is just asking for trouble.

Good Debt
Education
Real estate
Small business loan

Bad Debt (any debt that sits on a credit card and costs you interest)
Cars
Entertainment
Vacations
Appliances
Furniture

Credit Card Rehab

You've maxed out your cards and now it's time to get that balance down—way down! If you're home like so many other boomerangers because of maverick credit behavior, then you've come to the right place. Nothing says you're ready to make a clean start more than moving back home with your parents. In fact, it's a lot like entering credit rehab, in which you isolate yourself and admit to having a credit problem. After all, you don't want to pay for your mistakes for the rest of your life. Bad credit behavior can prevent you from getting cars, securing home loans, or even trying to rent an apartment.

Once you've taken that first but all-important step of vowing to improve your credit, you'll need to be carefully monitored to make sure you don't fall off the wagon. This section should help you stay on course and get off the credit merry-go-round so you can shrink that $10,000 balance to zero.

First Things First. Credit cards carry a far higher interest rate than your school loans, so prepare to pay off your cards first. And that's your goal, to start attacking the balance with the highest rate before you do anything else. Don't worry so much about the balance. A high balance doesn't mean squat when you compare the savings you're getting by paying off your highest-interest-bearing cards first. Once you determine which credit card has the highest interest rate, you'll need to double, and in some cases even triple, your minimum payments so you can really start making a dent in that balance.

The Fix Is In. Actually, there's no such thing as a fixed rate. Your credit card company has the right to hike up your interest rate as long as they inform you 15 days in advance. They may do this for a number of reasons, including late payment on your part. If you ask for a pardon, they may reverse the late payment fee, but still increase your rate. But credit card companies don't even need a reason. It's written in those really tiny letters in the standard agreement you signed. It's up to you to monitor your interest rate month to month just in case they try to slip something by you. And if they do raise your rate, don't be afraid to take your business elsewhere. Prepare to shop around and find a card with a better deal.

When the Minimum Just Won't Do. If you're still paying off the minimum each month, figure out how you can do better. Look, it's not like the credit card company is doing you any favors by letting you pay just 2 percent each month. They know exactly what they're doing and they're hoping you don't. It's like this: If you have a $3,000 credit card balance and you're paying just the $60 minimum payment, it will take you eight years to pay it off and will cost you $2,780 in interest. If you add an extra $50 to your payment each month, you'd be all paid off in three years and will have saved yourself $1,800 in extra interest charges.

Fight Fire with Fire. When it comes to credit cards, there's no such thing as loyalty. In fact, the really savvy players switch cards several times each year in order to profit from the introductory, ultra-low teaser rates dangled by each company. If a card is offering a low 1.5 percent interest rate for the first six months, you can take advantage of the low rates and then transfer your balance to another card before the six-month deadline is up. That way, if you keep transferring before the rate expires, you can benefit from these low rates until you pay off your entire balance. While it may take a few minutes to complete the transfer every six months or so, you can save thousands of dollars in interest fees. Since banks don't monitor how many times you transfer your balance, you can think of this as your way of getting even with the credit gods.

Negotiate a Lower Rate. If you don't want to deal with the hassle of transferring your balance every four to six months, you may still be able to haggle your way to a lower interest rate with your current card. To do this, you'll need to highlight your good credit standing and solid track record of repayment. If they still don't budge, threaten to jump ship to a competitor who has no annual fees and a lower rate. Most companies won't want to lose you as a customer and will match those terms if you seem serious about taking your business elsewhere.

Watch Those Fees. A dollar here. A dollar there. Those little fees may not seem like a lot, but add them up, and you're talking about hundreds of dollars that you could have saved each year. Credit card companies often pile on fees when you least expect it. If you don't pay attention and read the fine print carefully, you can be charged for any and all of the following:

- *A day late, a dollar short:* Besides hiking up your interest rate, some credit card companies will also charge you a fee if you're a day or even a few hours late with your payment. Of course, you can plead your case and offer an excuse. But your best bet for avoiding any unnecessary charges is just to send your payments on time each month.
- *Transferring your balance:* While playing hide and seek with the credit card companies may seem like a good idea and can save you tons of cash, you have to be extra careful to make sure your bank won't penalize you for shifting your balance to another card. So before you sign up, make sure to read the agreement carefully.
- *Cash out:* Talk about legal loan sharking. If you're thinking about getting a cash advance from your credit card company, DON'T! While your card may have no annual fees, once you've taken a cash advance, you'll be charged a 2 to 5 percent fee of your total cash advance. So if you're dire in need of cash, think of your credit card company as the last possible resort.

Credit vs. Debit. Since many of you die-hard addicts will have a hard time imagining life without plastic, asking you to cut up all your cards may not be a reasonable request. But why not start small? Since it won't be as painful as shredding your Visa or MasterCard, your first step is to cut up all those "extra" credit cards taking up space in your wallet (gas station cards, department store cards, etc.). Now that that's done with, consider exchanging your current credit card for a debit card. It looks and feels like the real thing, but is a much better alternative to credit. A debit card allows you the same convenience of purchasing items without cash or checks, but it differs in that the amount of your purchase is automatically deducted from your checking account. Find out if your bank offers a debit card and ask to be switched over. The trick with these cards is to make sure you have enough in your checking account to cover each transaction. If the store can't collect, you'll be hit with a fee.

Don't Give Up. When you're paying off your cards, keeping up with your payment plan is critical. So don't make financial promises you can't keep. That means you'll need to create a payment schedule that is realistic. If the most you can pay is $100 a month, don't promise to pay $150. While you may feel discouraged at first, small, gradual steps will help you pay down your card. Once you feel you're on a roll, don't let up on your payments. The balance can just as easily slide up as it can down. If you need to be reminded about your payment deadline each month, consider investing in financial software programs like Quicken or Microsoft Money.

Final tip: If you're drowning in debt and don't know where to start, you might want to contact a credit counselor. For a list of counselors, contact the National Foundation of Credit Counseling at 800-388-2227.

School Loan Hell

With the average college student graduating with about $16,000 worth of school loans, paying down college debt can seem like an insurmountable burden, especially when you consider how low most starting salaries are. It's enough to make even the most responsible boomeranger want to hide out in Mexico, or at least at Mom and Dad's house. Of course, defaulting on your school loan, no matter what financial dire straits you're in, is no laughing matter. Seriously, it can have severe repercussions on your credit rating for many years to come. Lucky for you, today's lenders are more flexible than ever. And that's good news for you. You'll find a variety of ways to work with your lending institutions in order to cut down or significantly reduce your monthly payments. Here are some strategies for conquering your debt.

Consolidate. Consolidating your loans is one of the most popular ways of reducing the monthly payments. Unfortunately, most graduates, myself included, have no idea what consolidation involves or that it even exists, for that matter. Basically, consolidation means converting your loan's interest rate from a variable to a fixed one. It could also mean extending your repayment schedule up to 30 years (which will give you more breathing room than the standard ten-year repayment term). But as with any too-good-to-be-true solution, there's a catch. It's all about timing. The downside is that since you can only consolidate one time, the rates better be at a good low percentage when you're ready to make your move. In the past few years, interest rates have been at all-time lows. Graduates with at least $7,500 in federal loans are eligible to take advantage of consolidation, and can extend their repayment period to 12, 20, or 30 years for standard loans. For more information, contact the Student Loan Consolidation Program by calling 866-311-8076 or visiting www .slcp.com. A loan officer will talk you through several repayment plans and will help you find one that's most suitable.

If you choose to go this route, you should also be aware that most school loans come fully equipped with a six-month grace period. The lenders want to give you enough time to find a job before you begin paying them off. But few people know that if you consolidate your loans before the grace period is up, your lender will shave an extra 0.06 percent off the repayment rate. In order to benefit, however, you'll have to start paying the loan back right away, so make sure you have the funds ready before electing this option.

Pick a Repayment Plan. You can rest assured you're not getting out of paying your school loans, but if you take your time, you may be able to customize a repayment plan that suits your needs. What many graduates don't realize is that there is more than one way to pay the piper.

> *Standard:* The standard payment plan (ten years) is for those who have found a relatively decent paying job and can make their monthly payments without too much strain. If you opt for this plan, you'll need to make equal payments for the entire length of your loan.
> *Graduated payment plan:* This payment plan is great for those of us who are toiling away at lousy entry-level jobs, but expect to make con-

ELINAFURMAN

siderably more money as we rise in our chosen field. That way, you can pay smaller monthly installments when you graduate and gradually increase that amount as you become more successful.

➐ *Income-based repayment plan:* This plan makes sense because it fluctuates according to your income. If you're making less one year and more the other, your payment rises and lowers in relation to your salary.

➐ *Extended payment plan:* Graduates who take advantage of this plan want to stretch the life of their loan to 25 years, which will reduce the amount they have to pay each month. To qualify for this schedule, the borrower must have received the loan on or after October 7, 1998. While this may seem like the answer to all your problems, remember that the longer you wait to pay off your loan, the more you'll end up paying in interest. In many cases, if you wait 25 years to settle your debt, you'll end up paying nearly double the original loan amount.

Cut Yourself Some Slack. Here's a lesson that will take you far in any area of your life: Ask and you shall receive—at least, some of the time. If you're worried that your payments are too high or that you'll never pay off your loans, never fear. A simple call to your friendly lender should ease some of your uncertainty. Your first goal is to ask about a repayment plan that works with your current lifestyle, financial circumstances, and future prospects. Once you pick out a plan that works for you, don't be afraid to ask for special treatment or to be informed of hidden cost-savers. For example, most lenders will shave 0.25 percent from your interest rate if you agree to have your monthly installment automatically deducted from your checking account. Bet you didn't know that! Another tip is to ask for a reduced rate based on good past credit behavior. If you've been paying regularly for three to five years, some lenders will decrease your interest rate by another full percentage point. So let that be a lesson to you. Companies may not advertise their customer-friendly policies, but if you ask, they may just let you in on their little secret.

Forgive and Forget. Even if you think you know everything there is to know about your school loan, you may be surprised to find out that Uncle Sam can wipe out a portion or, in some cases, even the whole thing if you volunteer your time and effort to a few worthy organizations. Not that you need to be bribed to volunteer, but it sure doesn't hurt to have that extra incentive. It's called "Loan Forgiveness" and if you play your cards right, you may just be granted a pardon.

- ➤ *AmeriCorps:* If you volunteer for AmeriCorps for one year, you'll get a $4,725 credit toward your loan and a $7,400 stipend. Call 800-942-2677 for more information.
- ➤ *Peace Corps:* Not only will you be helping your fellow man, seeing the world, and making new friends from one of 70 developing countries, you can also kiss some of your loans good-bye in the process. Peace Corps volunteers may apply to defer Stafford, Perkins, and consolidated loans. Perkins loans can be reduced 15 percent for every year of service. For more information, call 800-424-8580.
- ➤ *Volunteers in Service to America (VISTA):* If you volunteer your time to one of this organization's private, nonprofit divisions, you can trade 1,700 hours of service for a $4,725 discount on your debt. When you consider that you'll also be working to combat illiteracy, homelessness, and poverty, you'd be silly not to at least think about it.
- ➤ *Be All You Can Be:* If serving your country is right up there on your to-do list, you can make a significant dent in your debt by signing up for the armed services. If you're up to giving your life over to the National Guard or Army Reserve, you can get up to $10,000 to pay off your school loans.
- ➤ *Teach America:* Under the National Defense Education Act, graduates who go on to become full-time teachers in a school for low-income families can have their Perkins Loan reduced by 15 percent in their first two years of work. If you last two more years, that rate jumps to 20 percent. And if you make it to the fifth round, you can shave off 30 percent. To get a list of qualifying schools, contact your local school district's administration office.
- ➤ *Lawyers and Doctors, Oh My!:* If you're going to law school in order to champion the little guy, you may be in luck. For those of you serving in low-paying public interest or nonprofit jobs, the National Association for Public Interest Law may take an interest in cutting some of

your school loans. Give them a call at 202-466-3686 to find out more information.

And if medicine's your bag and you don't mind working in remote, economically depressed regions, you'd do well to contact the National Health Service Corps for more information about their loan forgiveness plan. Call 800-221-9393 for the details.

Deduct It. Good news! In 2003, you were allowed to deduct up to $3,000 in student loan interest from your income tax return. If you think about it, that's a huge savings. Of course, that number is subject to your income level. If you're making anywhere from $50,000 to $65,000 you may not be able to deduct the full amount. To process your deduction, watch your mail. You should be receiving an annual statement showing how much interest you've paid. But don't think this boon from the government will continue ad infinitum. You can only deduct your interest paid during the first 60 months of your loan's term.

GOAL 2. SAVING YOUR MONEY

Since I was putting myself through graduate school, living at home really helped me out financially. For the first time in my life, I could live stress-free and sort out my financial goals without worrying about making ends meet and paying rent every month. I figured out that it was important for me to be on my own and save an emergency fund. The most important thing I learned while I was saving up for my rent deposit was to be patient and grateful for the chance you have. It's really hard to save a couple of thousand dollars if you have to pay rent each month.

—Samantha, 27, Kingston, NY

The concept of saving is an easy enough one to grasp. In a nutshell, you have to spend less than you earn. Of course, losing weight is also a simple concept. You have to eat less to weigh less. But tell that to the millions of people battling the bulge—somehow it doesn't seem so easy when you're walking by a Krispy Kreme store. Much like going on a diet, understanding how to save money isn't enough. With so many tempting goodies beckoning you at every corner shop, only willpower can save the day. Let's face it, we're a culture of consumers. We shop when we're bored, when we're tired, when we're happy, and when we're sad. No matter how many times we try to get off the consumer bandwagon, somehow we end up right back where we started.

But saving money doesn't have to mean forgoing all your favorite things. No one's asking you to renounce all your worldly possessions and join a monastery, but you will have to become more aware of where your hard-earned cash is going. "Where does it all go?" Isn't that the magic question? Once you figure that out and curb mindless spending, you'd be surprised to find out how much money you have left over for your favorite things. Whether you're saving for an early retirement, a down payment on a home, or a nest egg that will allay your financial anxiety, learning to save money and watch your spending is a skill you'll need to master. Here are some tips for getting started.

Track Your Expenses

You've heard it a million times. Keeping track of every expense—be it your morning latte, a slice of pizza, or a new CD—is your first step to becoming saving savvy. Next, you'll need to divide your expenses into fixed and flexible expense categories to prioritize your spending. With so many fixed expenses every month (insurance, bills, credit cards, school loans), it's important that you know how much is left over for saving and spending every month. Here's an example of an expense breakdown:

Fixed Expenses
Bills (if your parents don't require a contribution, cross out this
    category)
Insurance (medical, dental, auto, etc.)
Transportation (train, car, gas, repairs)
Credit cards
Student loans

Flexible Expenses

Three-course dinner at Emilio's restaurant

Subscription to *Maxim* or *Lucky* magazines

Entertainment (movies, music, nightlife)

A Hawaiian shirt you'll only wear once

Five lottery tickets

A round of drinks at the bar

A $20 pedicure

Budget Wisely

Once you determine all your expenses, you'll need to create a budget. Here's a quick four-step breakdown of the process.

1. Calculate your total income, including any funds you receive in addition to your earnings.
2. Figure out your total fixed and flexible expenses (see above).
3. Calculate the amount you hope to save each month.
4. Determine if your income covers all of your current expenses. If not, then you'll need to cut down your expenses to fit your present income.

A good way to keep a tight rein on your spending is to invest in personal finance software, like Quicken or Microsoft Money. You can pay your bills, manage your investments, and do basic budgeting all in a one-stop shop. If financing software seems too complicated or expensive, you can check out some online budget calculators (www.mapping-your-future.org and www.free-financial-advice.net). These tools should give you a better idea of where your money's been going all these years.

Find the Magic Number

Once you figure out a basic budget, you'll need to figure out how much you'll need to save in order to meet your financial goals. If you're looking to save for a down payment on a house, figure you'll need about 10 percent of the total cost in order to be taken seriously. To get a sense of prices in your area, go online to check out the going rates for housing. On average, your first home will run you about, $100,000–$200,000. Do the math, and you'll see that you need to save about $15,000–$20,000 for a down payment. If you're saving for a nest egg, the common consensus is that you'll need about three months living expenses at the bare minimum, or about $8,000 to $10,000. Once you have a better idea of how much you'll need, you can figure out how long you'll have to stay at home to meet your goal.

Want Need, Need Not

Anyone will tell you that the best way to resist temptation is to resist tempting yourself. If you're out with your significant other and see a hottie in the corner, you'd probably try not to look, right? After all, there's no sense in torturing yourself. The same principle applies to saving money. The more you engage in consumer behaviors, like window-shopping, magazine browsing, and catalog ogling, the more you'll want the items you see. You'd be surprised at how many of our everyday activities revolve around browsing and shopping, teaching us to want things we never knew existed in the first place. But why whet your appetite when you know you can't have it? Burn your catalogs, delete all bookmarked shopping websites, and avoid malls like the plague. Believe me, you'll thank yourself when the credit card bill arrives.

I definitely moved home for financial reasons. I think at that point, it's what everyone seemed to be doing. A minority of people went out on their own, but the majority went back home. Considering the job market, it's not a rare circumstance. When I first moved home, I found myself spending a lot of money on girls and going to bars. I really had no idea where my small savings were all going. Finally, I had to stop and realize that if I wasn't going to save money now while living with my parents, when would I? I decided to take some odd jobs while a better position opened up in my field, and ended up working at one of those odd-job companies for about two years to save some money. Eventually, I was able to save up enough for a security deposit and moved into my own apartment. And while it doesn't

ELINAFURMAN

seem like much money to most, it helped me get back on my own.

—Greg, 24, Kew Gardens, NY

Live Large

Think you can't live the good life on a budget? Think again. All it takes is some creative thinking and ingenuity. If you love dining out in fancy restaurants, why not opt for lunch instead. You can often experience the same three-course meal at a third of the price. If travel makes you weak in the knees, think about working as an airline courier (check out www.courier.org for more information). You can often get flights for 85 percent off or even for free if you're willing to travel at 12 or 24 hours notice. Or, if you want to look as if you've just stepped off the pages of a magazine but can't afford the designer price tag, check out consignment stores in your area. This is where all the spoiled princesses donate last year's designer frocks in hopes that some less-blessed mortal will pick up their hand-me-downs. For a directory of consignment stores nationwide, check out www.consignmentshopsearch.com.

Internet Steals From travel to groceries to high-tech gadgets to cars, the Internet is a bargain hunter's dream. There are tons of savings to be had if you know where to look. But just because there are so many deals doesn't mean you'll need to take advantage of all of them. In the end, the best way to save money is not to spend at all.

HalfPrice.Restaurant.com: Here's a novel concept. Buy a $25 gift certificate at your favorite restaurant for half price (and sometimes as low as $10 or even $5) and then redeem at the restaurant for the full value. Just select your city and restaurant, and then print out your certificate. Of course, there are some restrictions. Some certificates require that you come in Monday through Thursday, and with parties of four or more. But with these savings, who's complaining?

CarsforGrads.com: Worried you won't be able to afford your own wheels? Freaked out about the prospect of carpooling with your parents? Don't worry. This website can help you find great deals on new rides. Created for graduating students and recent college grads just like yourself, it will help you save up to $750 on your next car purchase.

CityModa.com: If your inner fashionista is dying to come out, you may need to feed her need with some high-quality leather handbags. Whether you're looking for Fendi, Prada, Tod's, or even Balenciaga, you've come to the right place. Not only are these bags completely authentic, you'll save almost 60 percent off the retail price. Check out the Fendi Diavolo bag—that alone will feed your fashion urges for many months to come.

VistaPrint.com: If you're out of a job, but want to make a killer presentation at networking events and parties, you'll need professional business cards. But who can afford them? VistaPrint.com feels your pain and will offer you 250 business cards for the low, low price of $0. That's right, they're absolutely free! You can even customize your card with a design of your choice.

LowerMyBills.com: Not only can you sign up for their handy bill paying service and save hundreds in late fees, you can also do a comparison of all your monthly bills, including long-distance, cell, cable, and car insurance to make sure you're getting the best deal. Once you find the best offer, you can switch right then and there.

Hotwire.com: If you're looking for cheap airfare look no further then HotWire.com. Simply specify where you want to go and approximately what time you'd like to travel, and they'll come up with the best deal for your buck. Here's the caveat: You won't know when you're leaving or on what airline until you commit and plunk down a credit card. Seems risky to you? Don't worry. They only work with major airline carriers and guarantee no red-eye flights. So if you're worried about having to board Siberia Air at four in the morning, you're covered!

Direct Deposit

If your monthly paycheck is automatically deposited in your checking account each month, you'll have no problem with this concept. Basically, it's the same idea; the only difference is you'll have to write your own check. Once you've done the budgeting and figured out how much you can afford to save each month, you can automatically deposit that amount in a savings account. So if you decided that you'd be saving $100 each month, write a check for that amount and deposit it before you have a chance to get your grubby little hands on it. Not only will you not miss the money, you'll be thrilled every time you get a bank statement.

GOAL 3. GROWING YOUR MONEY

My parents have always been pretty savvy when it came to investments. So when I moved home to save money, we sat down with their financial advisor to come up with a savings plan. My parents agreed to let me live expense-free, so every month I pretty much put away everything I could in CDs. I started off with a few thousand and after two years at home, I had managed to save about $22,000. I'm only 24 now, so that's pretty much more money than I've ever seen before. When I moved out, I decided to put it away for retirement. If I never saved another penny, I would still have over $100,000 once I retire.
—Ashley, 24, Seattle, WA

All this talk about saving money won't mean jack if you don't know what to do with it. Take it from someone who let her condo proceeds languish in the savings account for a year because she didn't know what to do with it. Okay, so at least it wasn't sitting in my checking account, which is really the same as hiding your cash under the mattress. But still! When it comes to investing our money, many of us get confused, frazzled, and intimidated about the most basic investment strategies.

But don't be too hard on yourself. Your investment anxiety is not entirely all your fault. Very few of us were offered the option of taking an Investment 101 class in college. And even if you've picked up a few pointers here and there, you may still be confused about your options. The bottom line is that if you're going to make the most of your savings, you'll need to figure out how to maximize your funds. After all, there's no one investment strategy that works best for everyone. If you're not sure how to start and have a million questions about investing, you'll be well advised to check out some of the answers.

Why Invest?

"Saving is for chumps."

"Who knows, I might win the lottery."

"I have my whole life to start saving."

When it comes to socking away our pennies, many of us just don't see the point. We assume that the future will take care of itself, and don't want to worry about something so far off as retirement. But if you know anything about the sorry state of Social Security and want to actually retire someday, you'd be advised to start investing early. That's right, by the time we're ready to close up shop and reap the fruits of our labor, there might not be enough to go around. With higher life expectancy and dropping fertility rates, which means less people to support us, the National Center for Policy Analysis predicts that the Social Security fund will be depleted by the year 2030. Ouch!

"But why now?" you ask. It's simple. Investing money over time creates a snowball effect otherwise know as "compound interest." When Albert Einstein was asked to pinpoint one of the most powerful forces in the universe, he promptly responded with, "The power of compound interest." The man knows what he's talking about. With compound interest, the funds grow at an accelerated rate. If you invested $10,000 with an 11 percent return when you were 25, you'd have $650,010 by the time you turned 65 years old. If you waited ten years and invested the same amount on your thirty-fifth birthday, you'd have made only $228,920. So the earlier you start to invest, the more you'll make over time.

Even though retiring may seem like the last thing on your mind, you should definitely start thinking about it now. The longer you wait to start, the more you'll have to contribute each year to catch up. If you start saving in your twenties, you'll only need to put away 5 percent of your income. If you wait to start saving in

ELINAFURMAN

your thirties, you'll have to sock away 10 percent each year. And waiting until your forties, would mean that you'll have to put away about 20 percent of your salary to have any hope of enjoying your golden years. So unless you want to be the only grandpa/ma on the block with a paper route, your best bet is to start contributing to a retirement account as soon as possible.

Investment Reality Check For those of you still not convinced that investing is the way to go, check out this eye-popping chart.

If You Invest $10,000 for 10, 25, or 40 years

Rate	In 10 years	In 25 years	In 40 years
0% (Mattress)	$10,000	$10,000	$10,000
3% (Money Market)	$13,494	$21,150	$33,151
5% (Bond)	$16,470	$33,863	$70,399
11% (Stocks)	$29,891	$154,478	$798,345

What's My First Step?

Don't even think about starting to invest in the market until you max out your 401(k) or IRA account. While you won't be able to touch these savings until you turn 60, peace of mind is a small price to pay for long-term security. The benefits of investing in these accounts can be enormous. First off, the more of your income you put in to these accounts, the less taxes you will have to pay. If you invest $5,000 a year on a salary of $35,000, you'll only be taxed on a $30,000 income. That's a huge savings. Not only that, employer-sponsored 401(k) plans will often match your contribution dollar for dollar, fifty cents, or less in some cases. So if you invest about $5,000 in your 401(k), you'll end up with about $10,000 in retirement savings and with less taxes to pay. Of course, there are restrictions as to how much you can contribute. With a 401(k), you can contribute up to $10,500 and up to $2,000 in an IRA. But retirement accounts are still the best deal out there. You can even have your company automatically deduct a certain amount each month, and you won't have to miss the money. So before you invest in anything else, take advantage of this no-brainer opportunity.

Do I Need Short-or Long-Term Investments?

Good question! Your first course of action is to decide when you'll need the money you're saving. If you're looking to tap into some of your savings early in order to put a down payment on a house or are saving a nest egg for emergencies, you may need a short-term investment strategy that involves keeping most of your funds liquid. Liquidity allows you to cash out quickly without being penalized with heavy fees. In this case, your best bet is to invest in certificates of deposit (CDs) and U.S. Treasury and corporate bonds. If you're going to need your money relatively soon, investing your savings in the stock market won't make much sense since it can fluctuate dramatically from year to year. If you're planning for long-term goals like retirement or your children's education, then you'll need a separate investment strategy for that. In those cases, you'd be better off going into the stock market, since you won't be affected by any sudden day-to-day shifts. Better yet, you should probably have both short- and long-term goals, with some of your savings going into a retirement account and the other part toward more immediate needs like buying a house, going to grad school, or starting a small business.

What Is My Risk Tolerance?

Let's get one thing straight: the riskiest thing you can do is not to invest at all. If you don't invest your money in an interest-bearing account, you will lose more funds over time due to inflation.

When considering your risk quotient, remember that risk and return are related. The higher the risk of your investment, the higher the rate of your return. The safest investments are bonds, U.S. Treasuries, CDs, and bank accounts. These options are good for people with zero risk tolerance. Since these accounts are FDIC insured for up to $100,000, you're guaranteed to get your principal (original amount invested) back regardless of what happens in the market. The problem with these safe bets is that the rate of inflation often exceeds the rate of return. So in some cases, you may actually end up losing money by investing in these options.

If you have a medium risk tolerance, your best bet is to go in for a balanced mutual fund that invests in a combination of bonds and stocks. Over the long term, stocks have generated annual returns of about 10.5 percent. Long-term government bonds, on the other hand, have returned an average of 5.5 percent. Combining the two is recommended for those looking to minimize their risk and increase their return.

The key to investing wisely is to avoid anything that doesn't allow you to sleep soundly at night. You'll need to be able to ride out the year-to-year volatility in order to benefit from the long-term growth potential. So unless you're a seasoned financial veteran, steer clear of high-risk investments, which include opportunities like hedge funds, day trading, and futures.

Where Should I Invest?

With all this talk about stocks and bonds, your next step is to figure out how to best diversify and allocate your stash. It's the old "Don't put all your eggs in one basket!" rule. If you invest all your cash in one company's stock and it goes bust, there goes all your money. That's why so many people choose a mutual fund with a diversified selection of stocks and bonds. This approach significantly

| **Balancing Your Funds** | | | | | | |

Bonds! Stocks! Does it have to be so confusing? This chart is a good gauge for how to allocate your funds.

	Low Risk		Average Risk		High Risk	
Age	Stocks	Bonds	Stocks	Bonds	Stocks	Bonds
20	60%	40%	80%	20%	90%	10%
40	40%	60%	60%	40%	70%	30%
60	20%	80%	40%	60%	30%	70%

BOOMERANGNATION

reduces volatility and allows you to breathe easier for the duration of your investment. If you only plan to invest a small amount and can't afford the fees of a managed mutual fund, consider investing in an index fund, like the S&P 500, which has no fees and has reported about the same returns as managed funds on a long-term basis.

Besides investing in a mix of stocks and bonds, you should also keep some money in cash and real estate. Ideally, you should pick about four to six different investments to avoid risk and diversity your portfolio.

GOAL 4. PROTECTING YOUR ASSETS

For crying out loud, would you cover yourself? Just because you're back home in the safe confines of your family home doesn't mean something can't go wrong. Since some of you are home because of unemployment, dire financial straits, or other equally adverse circumstances, you'll need to be extra crafty about making sure your health, car, and possessions are well taken care of. And that doesn't mean letting your parents foot the bill for these costs. Here's a quick primer for covering your most precious assets.

Health Insurance

There's a reason why health coverage continues to be one of the most fiercely debated political issues. With millions of Americans going with insufficient or no health insurance, this is one of the most pressing social issues of our day. And boomerangers should take this issue even more seriously. One of the largest groups without coverage are 18- to 24-year-olds, according to Families USA, a health care advocacy group. Unemployed and self-employed young adults are choosing to go uninsured rather than pay the exorbitant premiums required, and who could blame them? I called several insurance companies (Blue Cross, Oxford, Aetna, and UNICARE) in New York City looking for a good deal. You can imagine my sticker shock when they told me that individual coverage would run me anywhere from $450 to $500 a month. And mind you, these were their most affordable and basic plans—no bells or whistles, nothing!

Financial problems among young adults due to exorbitant health care premiums, special noncovered services, and emergency room bills are becoming more and more common. So if you're not concerned about health insurance you should be.

Save for paying all your doctor bills and your monthly premiums, there's not a heck of a lot parents can do for us, either. Upon graduating college and forgoing your full-time student status, you can no longer be covered by their insurance plans. And when it comes to being covered by their employers, that option runs out when you turn 23 to 25 years of age. After that, you're on your own. If you've managed to hold down a job for any length of time, you're probably covered by your employer. But what if you're between jobs or self-employed like many other boomerangers? What are you supposed to do then? Here are a few options to consider.

Short-Term Policy. Since a short-term plan will only cover you in increments of 30, 60, 90, 120, or 180 days, it's a great option for the recently unemployed or those of you graduating from college. One of this plan's main draws is a low premium, anywhere from $30 to $150 per month. But here's the downside. With low premiums, expect high deductibles. That means you may have to pay up to $2,500 of out-of-pocket medical expenses before getting reimbursed by the insurer. These plans usually cover hospital charges, tests, routine office visits, checkups, and prescription drugs. It also allows you the freedom to choose your doctor. While these plans work well for most young adults, those of you with a preexisting medical condition may be denied coverage. Some good insurance companies that offer short-term coverage include Fortis, Golden Rule, and Blue Cross. To find a program in your area, contact your alumni association or search by state at www.GradMed.com.

COBRA. This health care option will work for those of you who are recently unemployed and are no longer eligible to be covered under your parents' plan because you've reached the policy's age limit. While this plan may buy you some time and will allow you to keep the health plan benefits you've become accustomed to, it's very, very expensive. You'll be paying 102 percent of the full cost in monthly premiums alone!

Catastrophic Coverage. If you're low on funds and can't afford a traditional plan, catastrophic coverage may be just the peace of mind you need without the hefty price tag. Basically, catastrophic coverage was created to keep you from going bankrupt in the event you end up hospitalized in a major accident. This plan will usually only cover lengthy hospital and medical stays, including related surgery, X-rays, and lab tests. You'll have a high deductible, anywhere from $1,000 and up, but your monthly premiums will be much lower. If you're always running to the doctor for checkups, this may not be the plan for you. But if you can't remember the last time you saw an MD, you may have found an affordable solution.

Freelancers Unit. If you're an artist, freelancer, independent contractor, work in the computer field, or are starting your own business in the New York area (one of the most expensive health care zones), get yourself over to www.WorkingToday.org. This site was started to give independent agents like yourself affordable health care options. If you qualify (e.g., earned over $9,000 in the last six months), you can expect to get a comprehensive individual medical plan for half the price of what you'd normally pay. Trust me, I know—after considering all my health care options, this was by far the most budget-friendly plan. For other areas outside of New York, consider joining a professional organization with health benefits to save big on your monthly payments.

Car Insurance

It's bad enough you have to beg your parents to drive their car every time you go out. But if you're not covered on their policy, your parents may not want to let you drive at all. If you're looking to borrow the family wheels, you'll have to talk to your parents about covering you as an extra driver. Of course, if you're only staying at home for a few months, you could fall under the category of "occasional driver," which wouldn't add any extra costs to their premium. But if you find that you'll be staying longer and using the car more often, your parents will need to contact their insurance provider to add you to their policy, and they'll have to pay extra to cover you. In some cases, adding an adult child with a clean driving record can add 30 percent or more to their monthly costs.

If you have your own car and are trying to figure out how to cover yourself for as little as possible, you'll need to contact your insurance agent. If you're moving from a big city to a smaller town, you may be eligible for a lower-cost policy. You may also be able to swing a special deal if you and your parents hold your two policies with the same insurance company. So before you do anything, make sure that you and your parents call your respective companies to find out who'll offer you the better deal. Visit Independent Insurance Agents of America (www.iiaa.org) for more information.

Home Insurance

For those of you who've lived on your own and actually applied for renter's insurance, you should be proud of yourself. Preparing for any contingency is the best way to avoid financial setbacks. It really is better to be safe than sorry. Now that you're moving back home, you should take every precaution to make sure your favorite belongings stay out of harm's way. When it comes to playing it safe in your new, albeit temporary, family home, make sure you boost your family's home insurance to include your personal belongings. Even if you think you don't need it, consider where you'd be if your laptop, stereo, or DVD/VCR combo TV got damaged or stolen. You probably have enough financial hardships to deal without having to replace all your favorite stuff.

Since your parents' home insurance won't cover your loss in case of fire, flood, or other major calamities, you'll need to take steps to insure your stuff. Once you get home, make sure to photograph all your valuables and make duplicates of any receipts you may have saved when purchasing the items. Since your parents' homeowner insurance policy may rise with the addition of your items, offer to pitch in a little bit to offset the extra expense.

A FINAL NOTE

I don't have to tell you that hashing out a sound financial strategy is one of the most important things you'll ever do. After all, if everything was so peachy in the personal finance department, you probably would not be living at home in the first place. Whether you're dead broke or just making ends meet, no one likes to talk about money. There's something about the subject that makes us all a wee bit squeamish. But talking about money is not important. What is of critical importance is that you *do* something about it. Doing nothing with your savings or just paying off the minimum on your credit card each month is a decision in and of itself. And a bad one at that, since you're actually losing money in the process.

So whether you're still in the red, wondering about the best way to sock away your savings, or just need to redefine your financial goals, don't wait too long to get started. It's never to early to start planning for the future. There's no better time than now, while you're still living at home with your parents, to iron out your goals and develop better money management habits. And while it may seem like the most daunting of tasks to turn around your financial life, it's not! It just takes sound planning, a little self-discipline, and lot of commitment to see your strategy through. Oh, is *that* all? Believe me, after surviving life at home the second time around, it's nothing you can't handle.

8

FRIENDS, LOVERS, AND ATTRACTIVE STRANGERS

When I first moved back to the suburbs after years of carefree college living, I hated my life. It seemed like everyone else was living this incredible urban tribe fantasy, complete with well-decorated coffeehouses, hot dates, cool friends, and roof parties. Everyone except me, that is. Here I was in the prime of my youth, working a meaningless entry-level job, and I had no social life to speak of. It wasn't fair. But I vowed not to let life at home deter me. So every weekend, my sister and I would make the perilous and long trek into the city. No one knew that we had come from the suburbs. But we knew the truth. While everyone else got happily toasted knowing they were just one cab ride away from home, my sister and I braced ourselves for the inevitable drive home. Cinderella had nothing on us. The carriage would turn into a pumpkin, the happy buzz into an irritable sobriety, and our formerly energetic selves into lethargic dolts.

—Elina, 31, New York, NY

A satisfying personal life can make or break your time at home. While it may feel as if you're stuck in social Siberia and that your life has become one long note from the underground, you'll need to work a little harder to make sure your social life is up to par. Boomerangers with a large network of friends and a significant other often find the transition to be smoother than their more isolated counterparts. Problem is, many of us find ourselves away from our former urban tribes and have to start completely from scratch.

Of course you could be one of those people who loves to be alone and is looking forward to the prospect of getting away from it all—friends, the dating merry-go-round, the late-night parties. And while the "I want to be alone" shtick may work wonders for a while, those of you who end up staying at home longer may find that you will eventually need to reach out and form new relationships. When that happens, you'll want to be ready!

If you're wondering how you'll ever manage to have a thriving personal life while living at home, don't worry. There are many ways of striking that perfect balance between being a lone warrior and social butterfly. And while you'll probably face obstacles along the way—parents, lack of privacy, few social outlets, a dwindling dating pool—this chapter will provide practical strategies for making the most of your boomerang years.

FRIENDS: WHO NEEDS THEM?

My social life wasn't all that great when I moved back home. I couldn't have any people over at my house. It wasn't horrible, but it wasn't like having privacy when you lived on your own. All of my friends were living in New York City at the time and I was stuck in suburban hell. I would have to drive in from Jersey to see them. It was a real pain since I had to bring back the car each time so my mom could use it in the morning. At first, I was a little lonely, but after a while I reestablished some friendships from my past and was able to hang out with them locally. I still felt like I was missing out on a ton of fun stuff with my friends in the city, but I eventually got used to it.

—Rachel, 27, Los Angeles, CA

Who needs friends? Well, for starters, you do! Your old coworkers, neighbors, and friends may have seemed like a huge pain to deal with, but now that they're gone and you only have your parents for support, you may miss them more than ever. That's the problem with friends: When you're dying for just a minute of privacy, there they are going on and on about their psycho boyfriend and dropping Pirate's Booty crumbs all over your couch. And then when you need them most and feel as if you'll go crazy if you have to spend another minute talking to your mom, they're nowhere to be found.

No one said maintaining our friendships would be easy.

There's just no telling why some friendships last a lifetime and others end as quickly as they start. Some we keep, some we toss. People move away, get married, get new jobs. There are a million reasons why we lose track of one another. It seems that every time we make a major transition, we have to start anew, knowing full well our new friends will never really replace the old. And isn't that what hurts us most? The knowledge that no matter how many new friends we make, they'll never know us in quite the same way. Making new friends begs scary questions, like "Who am I now?" and "What's so great about me?" And while figuring out the answers to those questions can be very beneficial, it can also be daunting and unsettling.

Making new friends should be challenging and exciting. But for many of us, the mere thought of hitting someone up for companionship ("Let's be friends!") fills us with the kind of social anxiety we haven't felt since high school. The older we get, the less open and adventurous we become. Of course, since you've probably experienced a million friend-shifts before (graduating college, moving to a new town) you should be well prepared to deal with your change of circumstances. Parting with the familiar is always difficult, but it can be especially hard now that you're heading home and have almost no idea of what the future will bring.

One thing's for certain: all of us, no matter how misanthropic, need people in our lives. Whether it's for emotional support, a reminder of how the other half lives, or someone to see the latest Vin Diesel flick with, friends are an invaluable part of life. And like it or not, you need them just as much as they need you. Still not convinced? Researchers Berkman and Syme studied thousands of Californians over a nine-year period and discovered that those with friends actually lived longer. So why not think of it as an investment in your health?

While you may be embarrassed, depressed, and feeling anything but social after moving back home, you don't have to kiss your personal life good-bye. In fact, it could be a great way to figure out who your real friends are and even reestablish ties with your old but not forgotten pals from the past.

Old Friends

> Since I've always lived at home, I have tons of old friends from my neighborhood. All my friends live really close by so it's very convenient when I want to see them or just hang out. I know my time at home wouldn't have been as easy if it wasn't for the fact that so many of my friends live literally a five-minute walking distance from my house. I think it would have been more of a struggle to stay at home as long as I have. And I know I would have been less happy with my situation.
>
> —Gina, 30, Astoria, NY

Remember little Susie, the one who stood up for you when you wore the wrong color sneakers? And where you would be today if wasn't for good old Billy, who got you out of more than one ass-whupping in high school? Even though your old childhood chums may be nothing more than a faint memory, they're still out there at this very moment. Who knows, they may even have had families of their own, gained 50 pounds, patented some great new invention, or done time in the state penitentiary.

Should Old Acquaintances Be Forgot . . .

In these highly consumerist times, it's easy to want to trade our last year's pumps, laptop, or handbag for the season's latest "it" items. But when it comes to friends, the new isn't always better than the old. Here's why:

- They don't stare at you blankly every time you say, "Remember that time we. . . ."
- They've seen you at your worst—think seventh grade, braces, baby fat.
- You don't have to tell them your whole life history upon first meeting.
- They already know how to deal with your parents.
- You won't have to wonder if they'll be there for you when times are tough.
- They won't judge you for moving back home with your parents.
- When you go out to bars, they can point out your type of girl/guy.

One of the most frequently overlooked benefits of moving back home is getting a second chance to connect with friends from the past and answer that burning question that keeps you up at night: "Where are they now?" With so many of us anxiously awaiting our high school and college reunions, you may just get your chance to take a nostalgia trip sooner. Even if you hated junior high and high school, you may still be curious about what happened to all those people. And while most of your old friends may be long gone, there may be a few still around. So if you're sulking about having to return to a small town or suburban digs, cheer up and remember to look up all those old friends you left behind. You may just rediscover why you were friends in the first place.

For whatever it's worth, hooking up with old friends from the past is bound to be amusing. Even if you decide that you're hopelessly incompatible or that you have nothing in common anymore, the sheer entertainment factor should be enough to motivate you. Once you've picked some prime candidates, pick up the phone and call. A simple, "Hi, I'm back in town. Want to get coffee?" should get the ball rolling.

The Old-Fashioned Method. What with e-mail, cell phones, and Blackberries everywhere you turn, there's something to be said for the trusty old phone directory. Pair that five-pound bad boy with your high school yearbook and you're virtually unstoppable. Just let your fingers do the walking as you stroll down memory lane. And don't just try to pick out people you were friends with before. Be brave and contact former students whom you may have always wondered about, but were too shy to approach. How about that ultra-mysterious dude reading Shakespeare in the library? Or that girl with the long dark hair who dressed like a hippie before it was cool? Of course, there may have been good reasons you weren't friends back then, but it never hurts to find out if they're still in the old neighborhood.

Word of Mouth. You'd be surprised how quickly word spreads when you move back home. If your parents live in a tight-knit community, chances are everyone will know of your homecoming almost before you do. While living in these gossipy, rumor-happy locales has some disadvantages, at least you won't have the burden of calling everyone personally. Who knows? Maybe your parents will even organize a "Welcome Home, for Now . . ." party where you can catch up with your old friends, relatives, and neighbors. If your town isn't about to throw a parade to commemorate your arrival, you can still get the word out by asking your family and old friends to spread the news.

Class Reunion. If you're nervous about making the first move, make sure to sign up for a free membership at www.Classmates .com for an anxiety-free way to reconnect. With over 130,000 high schools, elementary schools, and junior highs listed, as well as over 38 million members, you're bound to find some people from your past. Even if some of the other members are no longer living in the same area, you can still talk about the good old days or find out if they know someone who stayed in your hometown. Some other sites to try are www.Gradfinder.com and www.Reunion.com. It's a virtual high school reunion—without the fat jokes!

Current Friends

> My social life was definitely not the same when I moved back home because most of my friends didn't live close by. I went out much less than I did in college, which is kind of expected, but it didn't make me feel any better about my situation. Sometimes I would feel so isolated, and the only thing that got me through it was the fact that I was in constant contact with my close friends. I didn't even bother making any new friends, since I was busy always keeping in touch with my good friends from home and from school. I really missed them more than anything.
>
> —Amy, 27, Hoboken, NJ

Even if you've never lived the *Friends* experience, complete with Pottery Barn furniture, perky well-dressed pals, and goofy Kodak moments, you've probably made some good friends along the way. Whether they were your roommates, a core group of die-hard partiers, or girlfriends that you brunched and gossiped with every Sunday, there's bound to be a few people that you'll miss upon returning home. But just because you're bidding adieu to the residence formerly known as "yours" doesn't mean you have to lose contact with your pals. In fact, staying connected should be your first and foremost priority.

Besides the bonding, late-night gabbing fests and so on, one of the best reasons for holding on tight to your compadres is the all-important crash pad. Trust me, you'll be glad to have some breathing room from the parents. Besides this obvious advantage, your friends can also serve as your personal lifeline to the outside world. They'll keep you updated on all the latest gossip, invite you to parties in the city, and entertain you with stories about life on the other side. After all, there's no shame in living vicariously through them. It may even save your sanity. And who knows? You may be moving back sooner than you think. So why start all over with new friends, when you already have a ready-made crew?

Staying in Touch. What with competing schedules and the hectic pace of our daily lives, it's a wonder we're able to keep up with anyone at all. Hello? Is anybody out there? It's hard enough to keep up with friends when they live down the block, but now that you're geographically undesirable (GU), you'll have your work cut out for you. What do they say about being out of sight, out of mind? You guessed it! No matter how close you were with your friends before the move, even the tightest bonds can fade over time. That's why you're going to have to be crafty. Here are some tricks for staying in touch and on top of everyone's Evite list.

> ➐ *Don't Forget.* We've all been guilty of forgetting our best friend's birthday. Or it may have even been us that everyone forgot about (sniff, sniff). If you're going to give this friendship thing a fair shot, you'll need to keep updated records with phone numbers, addresses, and birthday information. But who has the time and energy to constantly

update one's address books? In fact, some of you are probably still keeping random scraps of paper tucked into a little notebook that you've had since high school. If you have any hope of salvaging your bonds, you'll need to upgrade your record-keeping system. There's nothing that can kill a friendship faster than outdated contact information. So what to do? It's simple. Get yourself over to www.Plaxo.com. Started by the guys who brought you Napster, Plaxo is an automated online service that securely and routinely updates all your contact information. Here's how it works. Your friends receive an e-mail asking them to update their information. They click on the link and are pointed to an area where they can edit and save their new information. That way, you won't have to do any of the work and the information will always be updated.

Another handy site that can save you much embarrassment and many guilt trips is www.BirthdayAlarm.com. Not only will this site send you a reminder of upcoming birthdays and special events, you can pick out electronic greeting cards to show that you care.

➐ *Visitation Rights.* Since you've suddenly become the odd wo/man out, take it upon yourself to act as the social coordinator of your group. Whether we're aware of it or not, there's always one person in every group who initiates the majority of the gatherings. Even if you've never been particularly motivated to get everyone together and were always the one who needed to get dragged out of the house, it's time to turn the tables. If you moved out to the 'burbs and all your friends are in the city, why not form a lunch or dinner club that meets once a month? Your friends can take turns picking the restaurant and you can send out the Evite.

➐ *Six Degrees of Separation.* Think the world revolves around you? Well, it actually may. In every group of friends, there's one person that is the main connector, the social glue that keeps everyone together. Usually it's the person who knows where all the best parties are, which restaurants just opened, and where all your friends are at any given time. Think of this person as friendship central, and your mission is to keep that person apprised of all your comings and goings. That way, they'll communicate the pertinent details to your group of friends even when you don't have time to keep in touch.

ELINAFURMAN

New Friends

Leaving your old friends behind was probably one of the toughest parts of boomeranging. Just when you got the perfect motley crew together, you're forced to start anew and socialize with (ick!) strangers. For you die-hard sentimentalists, the idea of having to establish new relationships can be as appealing as filing your taxes. But if you're moving to a town where you don't know a soul, that's precisely what you'll have to do. Remember, beggars can't be choosers!

One of the main obstacles to making new friends is our fear of being rejected. There's something about it that takes us right back to the terrifying first day of elementary school. But what happened? Okay, you moped around the first week. You may have even had to endure the mortification of eating lunch on your own, but eventually you made friends. And if you're lucky, you may have even maintained these relationships to this very day.

While some of you will embrace the challenge of meeting new people, others won't take to it as readily. But what's the alternative? Holing up in your bedroom and hanging out with your parents for the entire length of your stay? While they may be great and listen patiently to all your issues, there's something to be said about the challenges of relating to new people. And even though your old friends are just a phone call or e-mail away, you'll need the distraction of new places and faces to keep your life at home from feeling like purgatory.

Meeting and Greeting. Since you've probably been planning your escape since you got home, you may not be as motivated to meet new people, seeing it as a sign that you're putting down roots. You worry that forming attachments will keep you from moving on when the time is right. It's the same with decorating your room—just because it's not your permanent home doesn't mean you can't beautify it while you're there. The same goes for friends. Just because you think you're passing through doesn't mean you can't make new friendships that will make your time at home considerably more interesting and rewarding. Here are some tips for doing just that.

➔ *Virtual Friends.* By now, many of you have probably heard of www .Friendster.com. You sign up, your friends sign up, their friends sign up, and then their friends of friends sign up. The site is a piece of cake to use. All of you have to do is answer some questions about your likes, dislikes, favorite movies and music, and you're off and running. Suddenly you have a network of hundreds of cool new friends that you can hit up for advice, job leads, blind dates, or the occasional happy hour drink after work. If you're looking to form a large network and break the ice with new people, this website may be the answer to some of your prayers.

Another great way to forge connections online and take them into the real world is to sign up at www.Meetup.com. Whether you're interested in entrepreneurship, politics, books, web design, or Harry Potter—this mammoth website has the meeting for you. With planned events in thousands of cities and more than 1.4 million members, this site is a great way to find like-minded people in a town near you.

After I moved home from the city, I really felt cut off. I would get the "hey stranger" phone calls from friends in the city, but it was really hard to keep up those friendships. My social life went down the tubes, fast! The only new friends I made while living at home were the ones I made at work. I didn't really have that much of an opportunity to go out, so my only social outlet was my work environment.

—Mandy, 24, New York, NY

➔ *Whistle While You Work.* If you find that you're isolated and away from all your friends, don't miss out on the chance to form friendships at work. With so many of us using the excuse of full-time jobs to avoid meeting new people, it's not uncommon to mix work and pleasure. You figure, you're already stuck there for most of the day, so why not make the most of it? While some companies seem like one big happy hour, with everyone buzzing around and talking all day, others may foster a less congenial environment. But that shouldn't stop you. Even

if everyone is older than you or doesn't seem to be very outgoing, there are probably a few people who'd love to have a friend to make the day go by faster. If you're stumped for how to make the first move, consider asking someone in your department to join you for lunch. Or why not invite some people for drinks after work? Even if it seems that no one is interested in socializing, you may be surprised to find how receptive people are once you make an effort.

> *Join the Community:* Although few people take advantage, there are a lot of opportunities to get involved in your local community. Every town, no matter how small, has a community center. So why not use this chance to explore a hobby you enjoy and sign up for a class. There's yoga, art classes, and even book clubs. So even if you don't end up meeting anyone, you can still enjoy being creative and exploring your talents. Another fun strategy is to join a community playhouse. One boomeranger I know revived her love of acting by landing a lead role in a local production. Not only is she doing what she loves, she's made a whole slew of new friends at the theater. And finally, don't discount the opportunity to volunteer. It's the perfect way to meet like-minded altruists and remind yourself that no matter how bad you think you have it, others have it far worse.

SEX AND THE SUBURBS

It's a typical Saturday night. The girls are all decked out in their slinky off-the-shoulder black tops, their tiny lipstick-bearing clutches securely tucked underneath their arms. The guys sit huddled at the bar, pretending to watch the game as they sneak not-so-subtle glances at the girls. The DJ spins the latest hip-hop on the turntable and the drinks start to pour with increasing frequency. A guy wearing an Old Navy turtleneck and faded jeans stops a girl as she heads to the bathroom. Would she dance with him? Of course. Introductions are made and all the pertinent details exchanged. She's an executive assistant/aspiring actress. He just started his banking career. They both like to dance, German shepherds, and weekends on the shore. After a few more drinks, the couple gets even closer, making out in the banquettes at the end of the bar.

You're not antisocial. Check. You haven't contracted some strange disease. Check. So what's holding you back from getting out there? Could it be your parents? Even if you're very willing to meet new people, parents can sometimes interfere with your plans to have a thriving social life. It's not their fault, though. They may have the best of intentions, but just don't know how to act around your pals. If you're worried about your parents being a huge turnoff, here's a few strategies to help them see the light.

Spill It!: If you hate when your mom corners your friends to grill them about their love lives, then be honest about it. If you can't invite anyone over for fear that your dad will be walking around the house in his boxer shorts, warn him in advance. Your parents are not oracles. They can't read your mind as to what is and isn't acceptable behavior. If you're worried about hurting their feelings, preface everything with, "My friends think you're great, but . . ." They'll be too busy basking in the graciousness of your first compliment to be insulted about what comes next.

Include Them: Now that you've corrected the embarrassing behavior, make an effort to introduce your parents to your friends. Many boomerangers complain that their parents have a way of butting into their social time with friends at home. But parents only act this way when they feel that their company is unwanted. It's their own sad way of trying to win you over. So instead of fighting them, why not make an effort to introduce your friends and make some small talk before retiring to the privacy of your bedroom or basement. Once your parents feel as if they're not social lepers, they'll be much more willing to give you your space.

Be Discreet: If you and your friends like to party, smoke, and stay out late, make sure you don't aggravate your parents with these antics. Don't drink at home. Don't smoke at home. And don't invite friends over who do any of these things, either. While some parents won't mind you or your friends engaging in these behaviors in their house, others will prefer not to know about it. So keep it on the down low and your family won't be as liable to criticize you for hanging with the wrong crowd or other such nonsense.

From the looks of it, neither will be going home alone that night. So when the last call is announced, they stare at each other expectantly, both knowing what will come next.

"Let's go to your place," they both sputter in near-perfect unison. They laugh and then he tells her, "Well, my place is kind of messy right now." To which she responds, "Um, yeah, I have some out-of-town guests staying with me." Oh, well. They both smile at each other as if to say maybe next time. They exchange numbers and promise to call, as they sidle out of the bar and into the parking lot to find their cars. Waving good-bye, each curses under his/her breath as they make the long drive home back to their parents' house. Welcome to the world of the dating boomeranger.

DON'T ASK, DON'T TELL!

Imagine being about to close the deal only to be met with a look of wide-eyed horror after telling him/her that you're still living with Mom and Dad, and you'll understand why some of you probably develop hardcore issues about divulging this little bit of information. You can point to all the boomeranger statistics you want. You can talk about the high unemployment rate and the failing economy until you turn blue in the face. But no matter what you say, it's tough to get out those five little words—"I live with my parents"—when your sex life is on the line.

Look, no one said dating while you're at home would be easy. When it comes to this touchy subject, you're going to have to rise above all your hang-ups. While you may be tempted to cover up the truth, the last thing you want to do is start off a relationship, however brief, by lying. What if the person in question really likes you? What if he/she doesn't mind that you live at home? By omitting the gory details, you'll only be entangling yourself in unnecessary complications. And since the truth always comes out eventually, it's better to face the music now than risk alienating a perfectly nice paramour.

> I dated while I lived at home. I just didn't have girls stay over. Talking about living at home is not the kind of conversation you

want to have with someone on a first date. But if it came up
and I would get asked about it, I would always tell the truth. I
wouldn't lie, because they'll find out sooner or later and will resent you for lying. I don't think any of the girls I went out with
had a problem enough to stop seeing me, so I was pretty lucky.

—Wesley, 29, Nutley, NJ

If you've become gun-shy because of a few bad experiences,
you need to reassess and stop worrying about what everyone thinks
of you. Do I have to remind you that many of the people you're interested in are also living at home? It's the old case of "judge not,
lest you be judged." So if you're still stumbling around and looking
for love with little or no results, take heart. Living with parents and
having a thriving love life are not mutually exclusive. There are
plenty of boomerangers who have figured out how to avoid the
living-at-home dry spell. In fact, with a little ingenuity and a lot of
determination, you may end up having the time of your life.

STROKING YOUR EGO

As we all know, dating is nothing more than a confidence game; the
confidence it takes to approach someone new, make the first move,
and not get all freaked out every time someone rejects you. As a
young adult living at home, it's only normal that your normal self-
assurance is a bit rattled. The life of ease and luxury you hoped for
didn't exactly materialize as planned, and you may be shaken by financial and emotional circumstances that have led you to seek
refuge at home. So is it any wonder you're nervous about dating?

"Why would anyone want to date someone who lives at
home?" That's the question on every boomeranger's mind. So if
you're having serious doubts about your suitability as a suitor, let's
just say, you're not alone. Some young adults have even avoided
going back home for the sole fear that they wouldn't be "dateable"
once there. But as with most fears, this, too, is unfounded. Provided you make a little effort, you'll find that there are plenty of
people who want to date you, sleep with you, or just hang out with
you despite the fact that you live at home. And besides, there are

many hidden benefits to dating while living at home. Here are a few that you might not have thought of:

- **All about the Benjamins.** Some people are all about the right car, the right apartment, and the right clothes. But now that you're back to basics and living at home, you can tell who's really interested in you for *you*. It's a great way to start weeding out the phonies. So if people reject you just because you live at home, you know that they wouldn't be there for you in the long run. Just say "good riddance" and find yourself a more down-to-earth candidate.

- **Less Casual Sex.** Yeah, right! As if that's a benefit. Indulge me for just a second here. For those of you who've embraced the player lifestyle, the idea of getting laid less often is hardly a pleasant one. But consider what you'll gain from being forced to get to know your dates on a more platonic level before jumping in the sack. You may discover that he/she dreams of owning a restaurant some day, loves the same books as you, and has a dog named Benny that can do cartwheels. If you're used to picking up guy/girls at the bar and having all your dates end up in the sack because you just couldn't help yourself, consider this living at home thing a blessing in disguise. It may be just the thing to calm your raging hormones and remind you that there's more to people than one-night stands.

- **Family Values.** While some people only live at home out of sheer necessity, there are many more who find themselves drawn to the comforts of home. Even if you didn't appreciate your folks from the outset, you may have come around after a few months with the clan. Who knows? Your experience may have even reminded you of how important it is to have a family of your own someday. That's why you're such a prime candidate for all those marriage-minded singles. They'll be swarming around you like flies.

- **Quality versus Quantity.** Let's face it, while big cities and your old college town may have been teeming with one hot prospect after another, all those options may have spun you for a loop. After all, why bother settling down and getting to know someone when there's an equally if not more appealing option around the corner? There's something about being young and living among millions of singles that can

You only have one shot to close the deal. Whether you're mortified to admit to living at home or couldn't care less, hemming and hawing won't make your case any stronger. So when you're asked that one dreadful question—*"So, where do you live?"*—you better be ready with something quick and snappy. To avoid those awkward moments, try these comebacks on for size.

- **"I'm in between places."** Everyone can relate to being in transition. That's why this response works so well. Once you've admitted to being in limbo, you can follow up by saying that you're crashing at your parents' place for the time being. Your target doesn't have to know why you're there or or how long you're staying. Remember, a little mystery goes a long way.

- **"I'm taking care of my parents for a while."** Okay, so it may not be the absolute truth. But it could be. Many a boomeranger has moved home to help out his/her parents with financial and emotional issues. But even if that's not why you're really home, you can start living up to these words by doing a few things for your folks now and then. That way you won't be lying and your date will think you're one swell person.

- **"I'm saving up to buy a place of my own."** Even if you're only managing to save enough for gas and your weekly fix of Yoo-hoos, this response will work wonders for prospective dates who may be more practical-minded. The fact that you're saving up your pennies will make you seem ultra reliable and responsible. And all this talk about potential houses, businesses, or retirement will get them thinking about your future together—or at the very least, a second date!

- **"Where do *you* live?"** In dire times like these, turn about can be fair play. It may be obvious that you're avoiding the question, but you'll want to get their response first. If they answer by telling you that they live on so-and-so street, in that great new condo building, you can steer the conversation to how much you love that neighborhood and how you've always wondered about what the building looks like from inside. Hint! Hint! If they tell you they're living with Mom and/or Dad, consider the ice broken. You can breathe easier knowing you're in good company. Now the two of you can safely bond over the pitfalls of life at home while you secretly browse your memory for the cheapest and closest hotel room.

awake a commitment-phobe in all of us. And while you may have even dreamt of settling down someday, the idea of all that green grass on the other side may have kept you from establishing strong bonds. So why not look at the bright side? The lack of eye candy in your hometown can be just the thing you need to hunker down and form a serious relationship with someone.

HUNTING GROUNDS

In the past, you probably took the bounty of attractive and available singles for granted. Who could blame you? College and densely packed urban areas are gold mines of opportunities, so it was easy to think that the options would never run dry. Now that you're home, meeting people won't be as easy as putting on your shiniest lip gloss and venturing out to the corner deli for an egg and cheese sandwich. Oh, the good old days!

If you moved home to a smaller town, you may find that you're surrounded by more families than singles. Just as you're about to do your combination hair flip, wink, and wave, you find that the hot guy you were flirting with on the road was on his way to pick up his son from Little League. The horror! Note to yourself: Hitting on perfectly happy married people is a kind of a rite of passage when you move home. So don't blame yourself for making that mistake.

While it may seem that your new locale is lacking in dating options, you'd be surprised to find out how many young, attractive, and available singles there are in your area. It's just a matter of finding them. And while you may not be able to have as many dates as you did while living on your own, you may be tempted to spend more time getting to know each person rather than rushing off to find your next conquest. So where does a perfectly well-adjusted and happy boomeranger go to meet prospective dates? Here are some great places to meet singles in even the most remote locations:

Love Online

If you're tired of the bar scene and don't have time to troll around your neighborhood looking for singles, why not try online dating? Match.com, Eharmony.com, Jdate.com, and other personals sites are a great way for you to find singles in your area. Just enter your zip code and check out the profiles. It's like a catalog of available men and women! There's bound to be someone you're interested in getting to know. Once you've picked out a few candidates, you'll need to pay your membership fee and post your profile. With so many success stories of people meeting online, you'd be crazy not to at least try it out.

Safety in Numbers

If you haven't heard about the speed dating phenomenon sweeping the nation, you better listen up! There are thousands of speed dating services, but all of them have the same premise. You sit down, talk to 15 to 25 singles in variable intervals of time (three, five, and eight minutes), and then pick your matches. If your match selected you as well, then you're in luck. The company will send you each other's contact information so you can set up a date. You can even find events tailored to your age, religion, height, and parental status. With so many companies sprouting up in cities all over the country, there are bound to be dozens of events in your neck of the woods.

Local Hotspots

No, I don't mean your local watering hole. You don't need me to tell you that bars and neighboring nightlife are a good place to meet people on the prowl. But if you're looking for less competitive and low-key spots to meet singles, consider some of the following:

➐ *Car Washes:* All that time waiting for your car to dry may spark some conversation.

- *Grocery Stores:* Check out the carts to see who's shopping solo or for the family.
- *Video Stores:* All those movie options and aisle browsing should give you enough time to zone in on potential dates.
- *Library and Bookstores:* If you have the same taste in books, you may have other things in common.
- *Clubs and Organizations:* Young professionals, church groups, synagogues, and your local YMCA may have a score of single events in your area.

"YOUR PLACE OR MY PARENTS'?"

Dating was the biggest problem because I didn't have the freedom anymore to do what I wanted. If I didn't call my mom and tell her I was staying somewhere, I would feel guilty. Even if I did call her and she didn't like my boyfriend at the time I was home (which she didn't) I would get a huge guilt trip and feel bad anyway. There was no space for us to be, except for my room, where we could have privacy. It was very stressful on my relationships.

—Susan, 26, New York, NY

Ugggh! This is one question you hoped you'd never have to hear. But once you get over the initial embarrassment of confessing your boomeranger status, you'll need to come up with a strategy for getting your groove on. This is no time to get puritanical. A healthy sex life is an integral part of life. You wouldn't think of going without all your daily food groups and vitamins. So why would you even contemplate a life of celibacy? If you're planning to go without doing the deed the whole time you're home, you can't expect to function on an optimal level. Not only that, you'll be a huge pain to be around—snippy, easily aggravated, and stressed out. Think of your poor parents, friends, and coworkers. If you don't do it for yourself, at least do it for them.

For those of you with a steady significant other, you can breath a sigh of relief. Your libido is in no danger of getting on the endangered species list. Many boomerangers have reported being more satisfied with their living situation when they have a stable relationship to help them through. Not only will your boyfriend/girlfriend be there to support you emotionally, he/she will also be there when you're looking to get busy and blow off some steam. But just when you think it's safe to have sex in the bedroom, you may find out that your parents are anything but understanding. While some parents won't mind their boomerangers getting a little action from the ones they love, others will be weirded out by the prospect of you doing it in the next room, regardless of how long the two of you may have been dating. Of course, if you have the guts to pull it off, you can ask them how they'd feel if you barred them from having sex (and yes, your parents do have sex!) But even with all the reasoning and pleading, there's just no telling where your parents stand on the issue.

If you think getting a little time alone with your steady is difficult, consider that your parents may be even less understanding when it comes to bringing virtual strangers home. All of us know what it's like to be in between apartments and jobs. But when it comes to being in between relationships, we've all felt the pain of not knowing where your next meal is coming from. It's not so bad when we have our own place to live. At least then we know that the only limitations imposed on our sex life are our own pick-up skills. But when you're living at home, you'll need to reconcile yourself to the reality that getting some on the side will not be as easy as before. Not only could your parents object to the idea of casual sex on principle, they could also resent their house being used as your personal bordello.

> Dating was not really a problem. I even brought girls to the apartment while my parents were home. They were sleeping and the girls would leave before they woke up. Sometimes I would bring girls over, and my mom would complain to me about not doing that. I would apologize, but then I'd do it again anyway.
>
> —Lior, 31, Detroit, MI

Suffice it to say that if you happen to meet or are dating someone with a place of his/her own, consider yourself blessed. You'll be spared the tediousness of sneaking in late or fighting over visitation rights with your parents. But if you have no place to go other than your parents' house, craftiness will be the order of the day. Whatever your dating status, you'll need to come up with a practical strategy for finding alone time with your significant or not-so-significant other. Here are a few tried and true ways of getting some much-needed privacy.

- **Get Them Out of the House.** Look, it may be sneaky and underhanded, but boomerangers have got to do what they got to do. Whether you read the latest movie reviews from the paper to them each weekend or even offer to buy them tickets for being such great parents, you'll need to come up with ways to get them out of the house. Whet their appetite for recreation by sending them articles covering the latest entertainment and dining options. They'll thank you for being ultra considerate, and you'll thank me if you take this advice.

- **Join the PIA.** Being a part of the Parental Intelligence Agency means that you'll need to become a sleuth at tracking your parents' every move. To become a full-fledged member, you'll need to know where they are at any given time of the day. Not only that, you'll need to make sure you and your paramour have your watches perfectly synchronized so that you don't waste any precious time getting in and out of the house.

- **Quiet as a Mouse.** While some parents will ban your BF/GF entirely, there are those that will allow your "special friend" to stay over on one condition—that they sleep in a guest room or on the couch. Whatever you do, don't flip out. In parent speak, this really means "We don't want to know what happens once we're asleep." If this is your situation, you'll need to get really good at sneaking around. That means taking the time to noise-proof the route from the couch or guest room to your bed. Do a walk-through when your parents are not home to see which boards squeak the loudest, and then teach your steady to avoid them. Also, test your door for loud squeaking noises, and then make sure to oil the hinges to avoid waking them up.

- **Do Not Disturb.** Whatever moral or religious reasons your parents may have for not allowing your significant other to sleep over, your sex life need not suffer. I can't even tell you how grateful my now ex-boyfriend and I were for the hospitality of one Red Roof Inn. But before you start protesting on the grounds that cheap hotels are solely for the red-light-district set, consider whether you're in a position to take such a righteous attitude. Just because you need alternate accommodations doesn't mean you have to go to some sleazy motel, either. There are bound to be plenty of affordable, clean, and business-friendly hotels in your area. Even if you have to shell out $70 a couple times a month, it beats the alternative of never seeing your steady. And if you're looking for discounts, join the AAA or check out Hotels.com for deals in your area.

What Are Friends For? You've always been there for them, right? You were there when their cat died, when their boyfriend threw all their stuff out the window, when they locked themselves out of their apartment (for the third time that month!). So how about a little payback? After all, it's only fair. If you've racked up some friendship karma points, this is the time to redeem them. Don't go saving your favors for a rainy day. This is about as rainy as it's going to get. Ask them if you can use their place once in a while. If they have a spare room, great! If not, they could always clear out for a few hours while you conduct your business. It may be an imposition, but that's what friends are for.

The Last Resort. If all else fails and you're running out of options, you can always try to reason with your folks. Play up the sentimental angle by reminding them of their carefree days as a single. If you have a long-term boyfriend/girlfriend, appeal to their romantic side by explaining how much in love the two of you are and how tough it is not to have time alone. You'd be surprised at how understanding they can be, with some parents even offering to leave town for the weekend and others agreeing to look the other way when you bring someone home. Yes, just when you think it can't get any worse, it may get a whole lot better.

9

CLOSING TIME

I definitely ended up staying longer than I planned. At first, it was going to be just for one year. Then it turned into two years. I had a savings plan in place, but when I lost my job, I had no choice but to stay longer. Finally, I had to face that there wasn't much for me to do in my hometown. I'd need to go to another city if I ever hoped to find a decent job. But the thought of moving to a new place, where I didn't know anyone . . . that really freaked me out, especially since I had grown used to hanging around with my parents and three brothers. No one understood why I wanted to leave, which made it even tougher. Fortunately, I was able to find a job in the city before I left. It gave me that boost that I needed to get off my butt. Looking back, I'm much happier all in all. Even though I thought I was satisfied with my life, I think it was more a fear of moving on than anything.

—Glenn, 27, St. Louis, MO

Leaving

home is a huge decision! You've managed to save some money, bonded with the parents, made a couple of new friends, and maybe even gotten some more work experience under your belt. So why the long face? Well, you probably got used to a lot of the comforts of home. The thought of looking for a new apartment, packing up all your stuff, and changing your mailing address can seem like a huge pain in the neck, especially since you already have everything you need right here at home.

But as with all of life's many stages, this one also must come to an end, brave boomeranger. One of the toughest parts of life is knowing when one phase ends and when another begins. Some of the major anxiety we boomerangers face is constantly changing our minds and postponing our time of departure. If you're waiting for some sign from above, an epiphany that it's time to go, you may just be waiting forever. You may be packing your bags one day, determined to make it on your own, until Mom cooks your favorite dish. Or, you're certain you'll be ready to leave in a month, only to find out that Dad went and booked a tropical getaway for the whole family. All of a sudden, you beam with pride and wonder how you could have ever thought about leaving this wonderful group of people.

Whether you've found a dirt-cheap apartment you can actually afford, landed a new job, reached a milestone birthday, or are just ready to move on, living on your own again can be the start of something big. While some of you may be thrilled with your newfound independence, others dread the prospect of paying high rents, collecting quarters for the laundry, and living without the friends and family you've come to rely on. But whatever you do and however you feel about it, you should be proud of yourself. This is one step you won't regret taking!

SHOULD I STAY OR SHOULD I GO?: THE MOVING-OUT DECISION TOOL

Still have no idea if you're ready to move out on your own? Can't seem to pick that perfect moment to make your grand exit? It's only normal that you would have some qualms about taking this next step. But what's all the fuss about? It's not as if you haven't been on your own before. While you may have forgotten what it feels like to fend for yourself, it's just like riding a bike. Once you get back on again, it will all come back to you and you'll wonder why you were so nervous in the first place. This next section will help you deal with some of the fears and insecurities that can prevent you from making this all-important decision once and for all.

BREAK ON THROUGH

I know what it feels like to want to move desperately, but to feel as if your feet are stuck in a block of cement. And mind you, when I

While some of you may be ready to move on after only a few months, others will take years to get to the same point. After all, we're not all on the same timeline. You have to take your particular situation into account and realize that life is not a race to get to the finish line. While it may take you longer to cross over to the other side, you'll get there eventually. This quiz will help you figure out when it's time to take that leap.

1. You've saved up enough money to put down a deposit for an apartment.   True False

2. You landed a relatively steady job.   True False

3. You've long exceeded your moving-out deadline.   True False

4. You've found an affordable new living situation.   True False

5. You're dying to know what it feels like to be on your own again.   True False

6. Your debt is down to an all-time low.   True False

7. You just can't imagine another day living at home.   True False

8. You feel as if you've sorted out all the issues that brought you home in the first place.   True False

9. You've gotten involved with someone new, and want to move in with him/her.   True False

10. Your parents are beginning to drop hints about you finding a place of your own.   True False

SCORING

6 OR MORE TRUES You may have finally reached the tipping point. But remember, no matter how overdue your departure may be, take the time to enjoy your last few weeks at home. You'll regret making a hasty exit and not taking the time to appreciate all that you will be leaving behind.

6 OR MORE FALSES While you may be anxious to get on the road again and are tired of postponing your move, think about what's really driving you. Do you feel embarrassed to be living at home? Are you not getting along with your parents? Do you feel that you're losing your sense of independence? While all these are valid concerns, you would be wise to get your affairs in order before moving out, lest you end up right back where you started.

left home, I was really ready to go. I had just turned 30 and I felt as if my life was on permanent hiatus. I was depressed, just going through the motions of life, and not very motivated to do much of anything. I would toy with the idea of moving, but felt helpless and scared to change anything about my life. Something just kept me from doing it.

I kept making it more difficult for myself, and in retrospect I realize I was postponing the inevitable by making all kinds of outlandish plans. Like the time I planned to move to Spain, or maybe start a pet boarding service in our apartment. Or like the time I decided to move to Berkeley and get a Ph.D. in women's studies. And of course, where would I be without my exploratory trip to Portland? I flew five hours to see if it was a place I could live only to end up watching movies in my hotel room the whole time while it rained. Of course, looking back, moving on would have been as easy as renting an apartment down the block. But no, I had to complicate things.

When you're pondering the long voyage ahead, you'll run into a lot of hang-ups, glitches, internal struggles, and moral dilemmas as you try to figure out whether you're truly ready to be on your own. But don't get bogged down by fears and insecurities. Just stay focused on your goals, muster up your courage, and you'll be on your way out in no time.

Very Scary

What if my apartment sucks? What if I don't make any new friends? What if I hate it and want to come home? What if the world ends tomorrow? The future can be a scary thing. As a society, we've become so obsessed with battling our fear of the unknown that we've created a whole business revolved around fortune telling, trend spotting, and other predictive sciences. Unfortunately, there's no way of knowing whether you'll be ecstatically happy in your new home. But shouldn't that be the exciting part? When did we begin playing everything so safely? Isn't unpredictability part of what makes life so exhilarating? If you beg to differ and need some assurances as to what will come next, think about how your life has progressed up to this point. While some aspects may not have been to your liking, it's certainly hasn't been anything to fear, either.

Never Enough

After living at home and saving money on rent, you may have gotten used to the idea of having a disposable income to spend how you like. So the idea of moving into an apartment and plunking down between $700 and $1,200 a month could seem kind of scary. Not only will you have to tighten your belt and forgo all your favorite luxuries, you'll need to figure out a budget so you can continue to save on a monthly basis. But with all this talk about whether you can afford to move out, why not ask yourself if you can afford to stay. I have always put saving money and conserving resources as one of my top priorities, but at some point I realized that money isn't everything. What you stand to gain—independence, renewed optimism, mobility—cannot be measured in dollars and cents alone.

Timing's Not Everything

Ever heard this one? "When the time is right, I'll just know." Well, that's a whole lot of bunk. You can spend the rest of your life telling yourself you'll move when you finish writing your book, when you get back from your trip, when you get a promotion, when you win the lottery. When, when, when . . . Somehow it never seems like a good time to do it. Of course, you can't discount timing altogether. Think about how many events in your life have been subject to this powerful force. But timing can work just as much for you as it can against you. So don't think you have to pick the absolute perfect time to make your exit. Just pick your moment—any moment— and then make your move. It's as simple as that.

> After my mother left my dad for another man, I moved home to help him with the family business. He was really depressed, so everything pretty much fell on my shoulders. I had to do the inventory, bookkeeping, and handle the register every day. When I came home, I would cook my dad dinner and do my best to cheer him up. It was a full-time schedule. I had no time for

friends, dating, or any kind of life at all! At some point, I always knew I would leave, but I felt so guilty about leaving my father. After a few years, I decided that I wasn't doing either of us any favors. I knew his behavior wouldn't change so long as I was able to do everything for him. I really needed to get away and start a life of my own, so I applied and got into a Master of Fine Arts program that I had always dreamed of going to. When my dad found out, he was shocked. He couldn't believe I was leaving. He would cry every day and beg me to stay. But I told him that he would be okay. And you know what—he was! After a few months and some dark periods where I didn't know if he would make it, he started getting better and more upbeat. Last time I called him he was even talking about opening another location for the business. I really think my leaving was the best thing for both of us.

—Janice, 28, Philadelphia, PA

Parental Guilt

If your parents are willing to pack your bags, rent you a moving truck, and even give you some "good riddance" money in the hopes that you finally go, consider yourself lucky. You have no idea what it's like dealing with parental guilt trips. Save for throwing themselves in front of the door and crying every time you broach the subject, your parents can't really do anything to hold you back. But don't belittle their pain. While some of you have been mooching off your parents at every turn, others have made themselves an invaluable part of their family's life (remember, I warned you about this earlier). And while you can't be blamed for being such a good boomeranger, you've made your own bed. Your best bet is to point out all the benefits that your leaving will bestow. Now that you're gone, your parents can watch whatever TV shows they want, not worry about your comings and goings, and finally be able to reclaim all that extra space you were taking up. If they're still not convinced, reassure them that you will visit often, call every day, and continue to be there for them in every possible way—and actually mean it!

Indecision

Don't be the boomeranger who cried wolf! Constantly changing your mind about moving out will not only be draining on you, it may be equally as taxing on your folks. Of course, your decision isn't going to be easy. There are many positive and negative points to each alternative. In the end, it will come down to your gut feeling. But if you need to base your decision on something more concrete than feelings alone, try this system on for size.

1. Map out the decision you have to make. What are your alternatives—staying at home, moving to another city, another neighborhood, etc?
2. Collect as much information about each option. Research job opportunities in new cities, get advice from other boomerangers, etc.
3. Write a list of pros and cons for each decision.
4. Face up to any fears, hidden motives, or false assumptions that may affect the outcome.
5. Take a week to chill out and just think about your decision.
6. Stay or go? It's time to make the final call!

JUST DO IT! MOVING OUT PRIMER

In the end, after you've gone through millions of reasons and excuses, weighed up all the pros and cons, you may just have to take a leap of faith. After all, if you wait until you're 100 percent certain to do something, you may never end up doing anything at all. Take it from a reluctant kicker and screamer like myself. If you're even 70 percent sure you're making the right decision, then just go for it.

Prep Your Parents

No matter how anxious you are about the big move, don't forget that your parents will also have to make a huge adjustment. While some parents may breathe a long sigh of relief upon hearing your news, others will freak out and cling to you as if for dear life. The key to telling your parents is to do it as early as possible. That way, they have enough time to get used to the idea. But before you have the talk, make sure you mean business. The last thing you want to do is make them think you're leaving, only to change your mind again and again. Your parents have lives of their own and may not appreciate the constant back and forth.

Scope Out Your New Area

Whether you're moving crosstown, crosscountry, or even halfway across the world, you'll need to get the lay of the land before moving on. Research everything from nearby hospitals, safety issues, maps, public transportation routes, and bars and restaurants. If you have questions about local habits and neighborhoods, stop by www.craigslist.org and post your questions on the boards, or check out the city guides at www.egrad.com. You can also take an online test at www.findyourspot.com that will take your income, preferences, and lifestyle into account before spitting out a long list of cities that match your personality. Doing so will reassure you about your new location, and will eliminate some of the stress of the upcoming move.

Clean Out Your Room

As much as you hate the prospect of having your old room converted into an office or personal gym, you'll have to reconcile yourself to the idea. Your parents may want to use your room for any number of purposes, so be sure to clean it out thoroughly before making your grand exit. Throw out anything you don't need, remove artwork, and pack away all the items you're taking with you. Not only will cleaning out your room make it easier on your parents once you leave, you won't be as tempted to boomerang if you no longer have your old space to come back to.

Say Good-bye

Parting is such sweet sorrow. Even if you've been itching to get out of your parents home, you may experience mixed feelings about moving on. You can go from manic to depressed in the span of a few minutes. Leaving home, however many times you do it, is never easy. When all is said and done, you'll probably miss your parents more than you realize. After all, they were there for you when you needed them and will continue to be there as you move from one life stage to the next. That's why it's so important to say good-bye properly. Consider doing something special for your parents before you leave, like taking them on a mini-vacation or cooking their favorite meals for a week straight. That way, when it comes down to actually saying good-bye, they'll already know how much you'll miss them.

> I have to admit my parents put up with so much while I was home for three years. I was going through one crisis after another, broke up with my boyfriend, and dealt with all kinds of work problems. They were there for me through it all, and I know how hard it would have been for me if I had tried to make it on my own. Even now, I get tears in my eyes knowing I won't be able to have breakfast with them every day, listen to my mom's funny stories about her crazy coworkers, or tag along with my dad on his fishing trips. And it's not like I was moving far. I ended up finding a place a half hour from home. But I knew it would be the last time we would ever live together like that under one roof. I really wanted to do something special for them. I ended up inviting all their friends and some relatives over for a big surprise party. I can't even tell you how happy they were.
>
> —Blaire, 26, Boston, MA

Moving Timeline

So the big day is all set, is it? Now that you're ready to sail off, you've probably got a gazillion things to take care of. If you're moving out in a matter of weeks, you can use this handy timeline to keep track of all your to-dos.

Six Weeks Before the Move

- Tell your parents that you're planning to leave.
- Notify all your new and old friends that you're leaving and give them your new contact information.
- If you're relocating to a new place, don't forget to give notice to your current employer.
- Compose a list of all the items you want to move.
- Start researching your new neighborhood.
- Have a garage sale to sell off the items you no longer need.
- Call a few moving companies and get estimates in writing for your

move (ask about expected form of payment, since some companies only accept cash).

- Look into renting a U-Haul.
- If you got a new job in another city, find out which moving expenses your employer will cover.

Four Weeks Before the Move

- Notify your magazine subscriptions and newspaper delivery of your change of address.
- If moving long-distance, map out your route and book hotel rooms for your trip.
- Order boxes and start packing up your belongings.
- Check out health, car, and home insurance in your new area.
- Vow to spend more time with your parents now that you're leaving home.
- Start planning your going-away party.

One Week Before the Move

- Have your car cleaned and serviced for your trip.
- Pick up and complete your change-of-address form.
- Arrange to have enough cash to cover moving expenses.
- Clean your room thoroughly.
- Make sure to contact utility companies to have service turned on at your new address.
- Transfer or close your bank accounts if you're moving to a new city or state.
- If your friends and family helped you with the move, reward them with dinner and drinks.

Moving Day

- Plan to spend the entire day at the house with the movers.
- If you're going DIY, pack up your stuff in your car early in the morning.
- Take a final tour of your room. Double-check closets, drawers, and shelves to be sure they are empty.
- Hug your parents good-bye.
- Leave your keys at home. While some of you will prefer to keep them, others will be glad that next time they visit they'll have to knock just like any other guest.

BOOMERANGNATION

THE BOOMERANGER MANIFESTO

Hear ye, hear ye, boomerangers! As a group, our hope for survival is remarkably well forecasted. So whether you think that's good or bad, rest assured that this trend is here to stay. While you may be home for only a brief time, your departure from home is by no means the end of this saga. Not only will some of you be back at a later point in time, there will be many future boomerangers who will take your place. According to U.S. Census Bureau Projections, with Generation Y reaching adulthood, there will be millions more where you came from by the year 2010. And with the stigma all but virtually gone, you can bet that your younger brothers and sisters will follow in your furry slipper–clad feet in droves.

So what kind of legacy do we want to leave? What do we wish to convey to the legions of boomerangers that will follow long after we have moved on? For one thing, we need to consider how we, fair boomerangers, are going to affect the world we live in. What, did you think you could just mooch off your parents, forgo procreation, and the world would just continue as is? Don't be so sure. After all, our extended adolescence doesn't just affect us, our parents, and our significant others. Take Japan, for example. With millions of young women choosing to live at home and spend their money on Louis Vuittons rather than diaper bags, Japanese officials are running scared, worried about what this trend will mean to the population growth. And while the luxury market is going gangbusters over there, many other aspects of the economy are suffering.

But if you think this bleak scenario only affects our friends in the Far East, think again! With so many American young people postponing adulthood indefinitely to cohabit with the 'rents, it's not an entirely unwarranted fear. By not forming our own households and becoming good little consumers, we are adversely affecting the economy. Not only do we not invest in consumer durables or housing, we're also preventing our dear old parents from making major purchases and relocating due to their fear that they will have to support us indefinitely.

Another concern is that families are shrinking in size, and since we're waiting so long to have kids of our own, that age gap between parents and children is growing every year. But what's the alternative? Popping out a million babies and shopping until we're blue in the face despite the fact that we're faced with one of the bleakest economy and job outlooks of our time? After all, you can't be expected to do right by the system if the system doesn't do right by you. And that brings me to the final point of the hour. As young adults who've been hit hard by the social and economic reality, we could complain till the cows come home. But where's that going to get us? It's obvious that our pared-down circumstances are just the beginning of what will eventually become a vicious circle. We're overloaded with debt, so we can't produce. We can't get jobs, so why even consider starting a family? We can't afford housing, so we move in with our parents.

With the onset of adulthood now happening later and later, it's clear that policies crafted in the 1970s no longer work. With so many health insurance, tax, employment, and education laws based on the premise that young adults are fully independent by the age of 24, it's clear that we have to reevaluate the system. While I'd never advise you to assign blame without taking accountability for your own piece of this huge humble pie, there is something to be said for making grand-sweeping changes in legislation to help support the new generation as they try to launch careers, businesses, and families.

And while change won't happen overnight, being aware of some of the key issues, voting responsibly, and contacting your local congresspeople will insure that your younger brothers and sisters—and eventually your kids—will have a better go of it than you did. So in the name of progress and boomeranger unity, here are some issues you might want to take a stand on:

Health Insurance. I can't stress enough how important this issue has become for young adults. As soon as you graduate college and your student health insurance expires, you're pretty much on your own. And even if your parents' coverage still extends to you, it will only help you until you turn 24 years old. After that, if you're unemployed, self-employed, or an independent contractor, you'll have to dip into your own pocket for medical expenses or forgo the whole thing altogether—which is what most of us are doing due to skyrocketing premiums. We need to encourage our senators and congresspeople to extend health-care benefits to young adults who live at home with their parents.

Unemployment Benefits. With most entry-level job and internships lasting as long as it takes you to finish this book, Uncle Sam needs to seriously consider extending unemployment benefits to young adults who are just starting out in the workforce. If you only worked five months and didn't quite make the income requirement cut, you should still be able to benefit from some sort of support.

Financial Literacy. If we don't educate teens and college students about bad credit card practices and financial management, we could see millions more young people filing for bankruptcy and moving back home. That's why we need to propose making financial literacy courses a mandatory part of the high school and university curriculums. This subject has to be at least as important as wood shop!

Tax Relief. Since many of your parents are still supporting you well into your late twenties shouldn't they be entitled to some tax relief? As it stands now, you stop being a dependent when you turn 19 years old, or 24 if you're a full-time student. But as we all know, it takes much longer than that to become fully autonomous. Shouldn't parents supporting boomerangers with little to no income at least get a small tax break? I think so.

Education Reform. The Pell Grant has been hit hard. With so many dollars that could have gone to underprivileged kids, there's no excuses for cutting student aid and taxing young people who want to go to school. We need to make our voices heard in support of the Federal College Scholarship, or Pell Grant, and fight against the tuition increases that will stop millions from getting the education they deserve. Not only that, with many young adults going into debt because of an extended six-year graduation cycle, we need to encourage young adults to graduate on time by introducing rules that limit the number of years one could attend school. And finally, we need to fight for tax relief in the form of a college opportunity tax credit, which would provide more significant tax deductions for parents and young adults who are paying for college.

Entry-Level Jobs. If you haven't heard, the United States is losing jobs by the tens of thousands. And whatever new jobs are created aren't sufficient to meet the needs of us boomerangers. We need to incite our government to create jobs that will give us a leg up instead of just tide us over. You didn't earn a degree in economics just so you could count change at the Starbucks counter. To this end, let's propose that our government provide tax credits to corporations that create new entry-level jobs for recent graduates.

Housing. With starter homes selling for $200,000 on average and renting costs rising astronomically, we need to do some serious thinking about how to provide young adults with adequate housing options. These days, it's almost impossible to support ourselves and still be able to afford a place of our own. And if we're not provided low-cost housing options, our lack of residential autonomy is bound to have an adverse impact on society as a whole.

Credit Reform. Since we know credit card companies aren't going to go out of business anytime soon, we need to think about how to create responsible credit behavior in the next generation. Some ideas include introducing a bill that would limit the amount of credit college students can assume, and one that would also require parental approval on any new credit card application. After all, credit should be a right, not a privilege.

IN CONCLUSION

Is this the end? Well, that all depends on how you look at it. There's no doubt you've been through a lot in your lifetime. The breakups, the careers, the tattoos, the crappy apartments, the wildly fluctuating incomes. Who knows? You may have even lost and made a million dollars in your lifetime—even if it *was* only on paper. And for all the comings and goings, for all your disappointments and victories, you can bet that no matter how much you've gone through, this is still just the beginning.

Having landed on your parents' doorstep, you've probably had your share of battle stories from the home front. Your parents may have driven you crazy with their constant complaints, pestered you about your nose ring, and chased you through the house demanding an explanation as to how a condom wrapper got into the upstairs bathroom. Some of you may also have had the time of your life as you discovered that it's okay to drink with your parents, that your siblings aren't really evil, and that life doesn't always work out according to plan—and that that's okay!

But whatever your particular experience, hopefully all of you benefited from this book. If nothing else, by reading the stories of people who've been there and survived, the one thing you should walk away knowing is that for all your doubts, worries, and insecurities, you're in good company.

Even if you're nowhere close to moving out and are just arriving home for the first time, it's all ahead of you. Treat everything as if you're seeing it for the first time, don't make assumptions, and forget everything you've learned or think you know about your parents. Because no matter how things seem right now, you're not moving backward and you're not standing still. Living at home isn't purgatory, it's your life and it's happening now!

In the end, it's not your finances, your relationship problems, or your job woes that are important, but what you take out of and put into this experience. So whether you leave home in a blaze of glory vowing never to return or barely manage to crawl out of the warm cocoon with your autonomy intact, remember the laws of karma. Because one day when you least expect it, when you're at your most commitment-phobic, when you're looking left instead of right, you may just start a family and have kids of your own. Kids that may someday come home again. And when that day comes, for God's sakes, people, change the locks!

ACKNOWLEDGMENTS

With so many people to thank, where to begin? First of, I would like to express thanks to all of you—the boomerangers—who have bravely forged a path that defies convention, expectations, and oftentimes logic. The stories, honesty, and wisdom you shared with me gave me all the inspiration I needed to tackle this subject. Your optimism, faith, and determination in the face of so much uncertainty inspired me to view my own experiences in a completely different way. And for that, you'll always be first in my book.

Much gratitude to my agent, Laurie Abkemeier, who fought for this book every step of the way. I can't express how ecstatic I am to have found an agent as talented, hardworking, honest, and dedicated as Laurie. Every author should be so lucky!

To my editor, Amanda Patten, whose sense of humor, keen editorial judgment, and unwavering belief in this project kept me motivated and on track.

To my sister, Leah, a wonderful writer and person. Thanks for keeping me company all those years.

To my research assistants, Rebecca and Carolena. Thank you for all your hard work!

Much appreciation to friends past and present, thanks! You know who you are.

And finally, all my love and gratitude to Jay. I couldn't have done it without you—and nor would I ever want to.